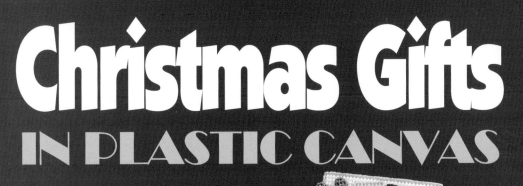

Christmas Gifts
IN PLASTIC CANVAS

Get ready to spread an abundance of holiday cheer with handmade gifts from the heart! In this volume of eye-catching plastic canvas creations, you'll find wonderful ideas for everyone on your list — from Baby to Grandma. Choose the most festive Yuletide projects, or select notions that can be used all year round. May this magical time be filled with the joy of sharing!

LEISURE ARTS, INC.
and
OXMOOR HOUSE, INC.

Christmas Gifts
IN PLASTIC CANVAS

EDITORIAL STAFF

Vice President and Editor-in-Chief:
Anne Van Wagner Childs
Executive Director: Sandra Graham Case
Editorial Director: Susan Frantz Wiles
Publications Directors: Carla Bentley
and Susan White Sullivan
Creative Art Director: Gloria Bearden
Senior Graphics Art Director: Melinda Stout

PRODUCTION
Special Projects Editor: Donna Brown Hill
Senior Production Assistant: JoAnn Dickson Forrest

EDITORIAL
Managing Editor: Linda L. Trimble
Associate Editor: Stacey Robertson Marshall
Assistant Editors: Terri Leming Davidson and
Janice Teipen Wojcik

ART
Crafts Art Director: Rhonda Hodge Shelby
Senior Production Artist: Katie Murphy
Production Artists: Brent Miller, Lora Puls,
Mindy Reynolds, Dana Vaughn, and Karen L. Wilson
Photography Stylists: Beth Carter, Ellen J. Clifton,
and Aurora Huston

PROMOTIONS
Managing Editor: Alan Caudle
Associate Editor: Steve M. Cooper
Art Director: Linda Lovette Smart
Publishing Systems Administrator: Cindy Lumpkin
Publishing Systems Assistant: Myra Means

BUSINESS STAFF

Publisher: Rick Barton
Vice President and General Manager: Thomas L. Carlisle
Vice President, Finance: Tom Siebenmorgen
Vice President, Retail Marketing: Bob Humphrey
Vice President, National Accounts: Pam Stebbins
Retail Marketing Director: Margaret Sweetin
General Merchandise Manager: Cathy Laird

Vice President, Operations: Brian U. Davis
Distribution Director: Rob Thieme
Retail Customer Service Director: Tonie B. Maulding
Retail Customer Service Managers: Carolyn Pruss and
Wanda Price
Print Production Manager: Fred F. Pruss

Library of Congress Catalog Number 98-75653
Hardcover ISBN 1-57486-130-1
Softcover ISBN 1-57486-131-X

10 9 8 7 6 5 4 3 2 1

TABLE OF CONTENTS

Snowy Day Coaster Set

This broom-toting snowman is ready to warm up chilly winter days for your favorite folks. Our adorable friend makes a cute holder for handy mitten coasters that are stitched to look like they're really knitted!

SNOWY DAY COASTER SET

Box Size: 4"w x 5"h x 2¼"d

Coaster Size: 4"w x 4¼"h

Supplies: Worsted weight yarn, embroidery floss, two 10½" x 13½" sheets of clear 7 mesh plastic canvas, #16 tapestry needle, cork or felt (optional), and craft glue

Stitches Used: Backstitch, French Knot, Gobelin Stitch, Overcast Stitch, and Tent Stitch

Instructions: Follow charts to cut and stitch pieces. Using white yarn, join Box Front to Sides. Join Back to Sides. Join Bottom to Front, Back, and Sides. Glue Nose, Broom, and Arm to Box Front. If desired, cut a piece of cork or felt slightly smaller than each Coaster. Glue cork or felt to back of Coasters.

Design by Michele Wilcox.

	COLOR	NL#	DMC#
	white	41	
	gold	11	
	orange	52	
	red	01	
	brown	13	
	desired color		
	desired color		
	red floss		304
	black floss		310
●	black floss French Knot		310

Nose
(6 x 7 threads)

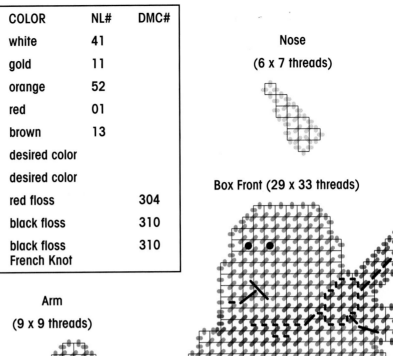

Box Front (29 x 33 threads)

Arm
(9 x 9 threads)

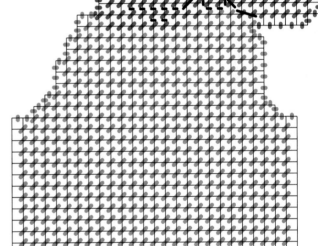

Box Side

(14 x 13 threads) (stitch 2)

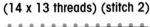
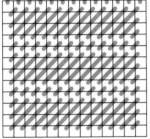

Box Back (27 x 13 threads)

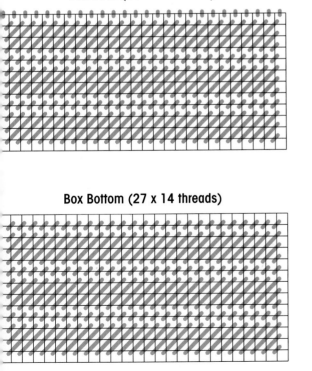

Box Bottom (27 x 14 threads)

Broom
(8 x 28 threads)

Coaster (26 x 28 threads) (stitch 6)

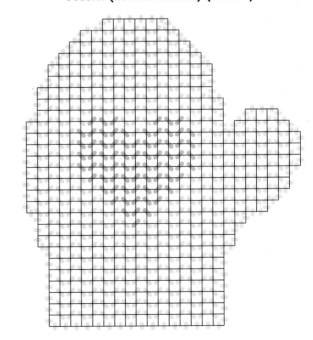

5

Saving for a rainy day can be fun with this nifty bank for kids! Stitched with vibrant yarn and topped with a bright red pom-pom, our perky fellow will cheer up any child's room.

CLOWNING AROUND

Size: 4¼"w x 7½"h x 2"d

Supplies: Worsted weight yarn, two 10½" x 13½" sheets of clear 7 mesh plastic canvas, #16 tapestry needle, 1" red pom-pom, and craft glue

Stitches Used: Backstitch, French Knot, Fringe Stitch, Gobelin Stitch, Mosaic Stitch, Overcast Stitch, Scotch Stitch, and Tent Stitch

Instructions: Follow charts to cut and stitch pieces. Trim Fringe on Bank Front to ½" long. Trim Fringe on Head Side pieces and Bank Back to 1" long.
Using green yarn, join Bank Sides to Bank Front along long edges of Front. Join Back to Sides.
Using flesh yarn, join Head Side pieces to Bank Front and Back. Using green yarn, join Shoulder pieces to Bank Front, Bank Sides, Bank Back, and Head Sides.
Using white yarn, join Hat Front to Hat Side pieces. Join Hat Sides to Hat Back. Join Hat Side pieces together.
For Bottom, cut two pieces of plastic canvas 28 x 6 threads each. Bottom is not stitched. Overlap long edges of Bottom pieces two threads and tack together. Using green yarn, join Bottom pieces to Bank Front, Sides, and Back. To remove coins from Bank, cut yarn used to tack Bottom together and squeeze Bank Sides to separate Bottom pieces.
Glue Bow Tie and pom-pom to Bank.

Design by Maryanne Moreck.

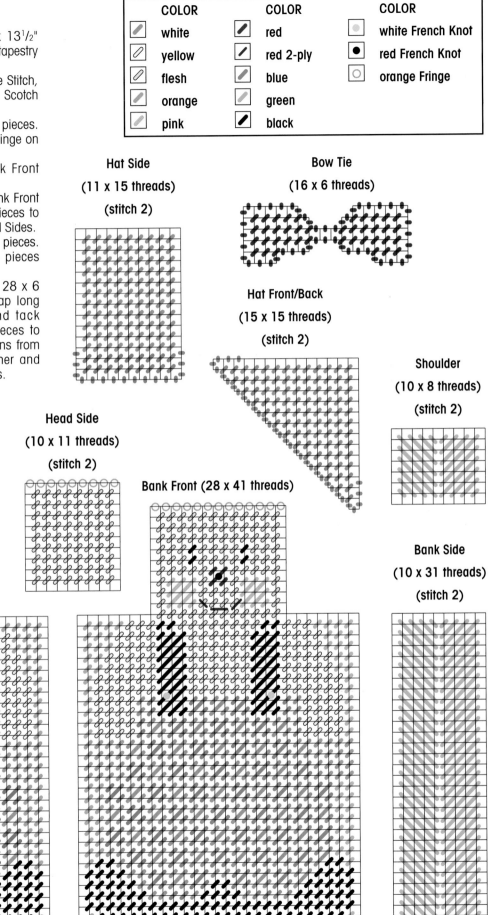

Hat Side
(11 x 15 threads)
(stitch 2)

Bow Tie
(16 x 6 threads)

Hat Front/Back
(15 x 15 threads)
(stitch 2)

Shoulder
(10 x 8 threads)
(stitch 2)

Head Side
(10 x 11 threads)
(stitch 2)

Bank Back (28 x 41 threads)

Bank Front (28 x 41 threads)

Bank Side
(10 x 31 threads)
(stitch 2)

Cup Of Cheer

Share a warming holiday sentiment with this creative teacup magnet. Tuck a real teabag inside the cup and add a heartfelt message for a unique gift.

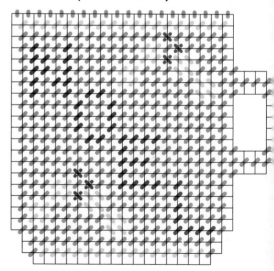

CUP OF CHEER

Size: 3³/₄"w x 3¹/₄"h x ¹/₂"d

Supplies: Worsted weight yarn, one 10¹/₂" x 13¹/₂" sheet of clear 7 mesh plastic canvas, #16 tapestry needle, magnetic strip, craft glue, and tea bag or potpourri (if desired)

Stitches Used: Cross Stitch, Overcast Stitch, and Tent Stitch

Instructions: Follow chart to cut and stitch Front. For Back, cut a Front piece, turn piece over, and cover with white Tent Stitches.

Using white yarn, cover unworked top edge of Back. Join remaining unworked edges of Front to Back. Glue magnetic strip to Teacup. If desired, insert tea bag or potpourri into Teacup.

Design by Fran Way Bohler.

	COLOR	NL#
/	white	41
/	red	02
/	green	27

Teacup Front

(25 x 23 threads)

Snowman Surprise

*This dapper snowman has a secret —
his hat tops off a "recycled" potato chip
canister! The easy project makes a clever
way to carry treats to a friend or neighbor.*

SNOWMAN SURPRISE

Size: 5"w x 4³/₄"h x 4³/₄"d
(Fits a 3³/₄"h x 3" dia. potato chip can.)

Supplies: Worsted weight yarn, one 10¹/₂" x 13¹/₂" sheet of clear 7 mesh plastic canvas, Darice® 6" dia. plastic canvas circle, #16 tapestry needle, and craft glue

Stitches Used: Alternating Scotch Stitch, Cross Stitch, Gobelin Stitch, Mosaic Stitch, Overcast Stitch, Scotch Stitch, and Tent Stitch

Instructions: Follow charts to cut Snowman and Hat Side pieces. Refer to chart to cut Hat Brim from plastic canvas circle along blue cutting lines. Cut Hat Top along pink cutting line. Follow charts to stitch pieces, leaving stitches in pink shaded areas unworked.

Using matching color yarn, join Snowman together along unworked edges to form a cylinder.

Matching ▲'s, overlap canvas and work pink shaded stitches to join Hat Side together, forming a cylinder. Using black yarn, join Brim to Side. Join Top to Side. Cover unworked edges of Brim.

Glue Eye and Mouth pieces to Snowman. Using green yarn, tack Scarf pieces to Snowman. Using orange yarn, tack Nose to Snowman. Using black yarn, bend Hat Brim and tack in place. Glue Flower pieces together. Tack Flower to Hat.

Design by MizFitz.

	COLOR	NL#
◢	white	41
◢	yellow	57
◢	orange	58
◢	pink	07
◢	red	01
◢	green	29
◢	brown	15
◢	black	00
○	red Fringe	01
○	green Fringe	29

Mouth

(3 x 3 threads)

(stitch 5)

Eyes

(4 x 4 threads)

(stitch 2)

Nose

(7 x 4 threads)

Hat Brim/Hat Top

Scarf Top

(5 x 11 threads)

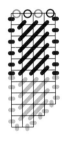

Scarf Bottom

(13 x 5 threads)

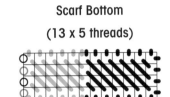

Flower Center

(5 x 5 threads)

Flower

(9 x 9 threads)

(stitch 2)

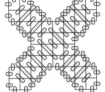

Hat Side (75 x 12 threads)

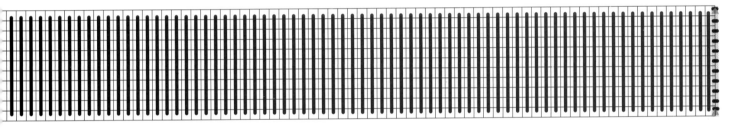

Snowman (67 x 25 threads)

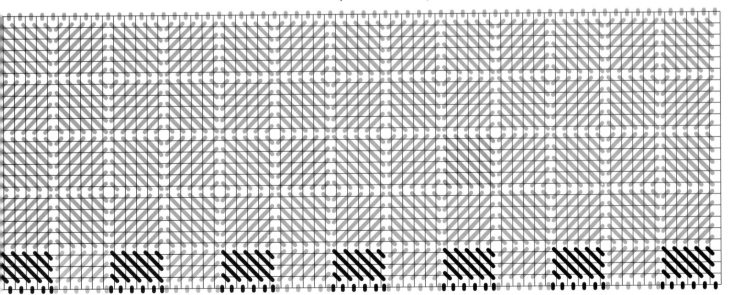

Personal Charms

Resembling the popular silver jewelry that commemorates birthdates and anniversaries, our tiny charms make wonderfully personal gifts. Metallic embroidery floss brings luster to the 14 mesh canvas creations, which feature colored jewels to signify the special months being celebrated.

BIRTHSTONE COLORS

● January - Garnet	● July - Ruby
● February - Amethyst	● August - Peridot
○ March - Aquamarine	● September - Sapphire
○ April - Diamond	● October - Tourmaline
● May - Emerald	○ November - Topaz
○ June - Alexandrite	● December - Turquoise

PERSONAL CHARMS

Anniversary Charm Size: 1¼"w x 1¼"h
Boy and Girl Charm Size: ¾"w x 1"h each
Pin Supplies: Silver DMC Embroidery Floss, one 8" x 11" sheet of clear 14 mesh plastic canvas, #24 tapestry needle, ¾" pin back, 4mm pony bead for each Charm, and craft glue
Necklace Supplies: Silver DMC Embroidery Floss, one 8" x 11" sheet of clear 14 mesh plastic canvas, #24 tapestry needle, 4mm pony bead for each Charm, 6mm silver round jump ring for each charm, 18" silver chain, and clear 6mm x 9mm pony beads
Stitches Used: Gobelin Stitch, Overcast Stitch, and Tent Stitch
Instructions: Follow chart to cut and stitch desired design using three strands of embroidery floss. Thread three strands of embroidery floss through hole on birthstone bead; run threads under the back of a few stitches on Charm to place bead in center of Charm.
For Pin, glue pin back to Charm.
For Necklace, attach silver jump ring to each Charm. Alternate Charms and clear pony beads on chain as shown in photo.

Designs by Becky Dill.

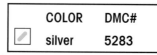

	COLOR	DMC#
⬜	silver	5283

Boy Charm
(10 x 13 threads)

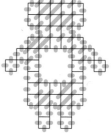

Anniversary Charm
(18 x 17 threads)

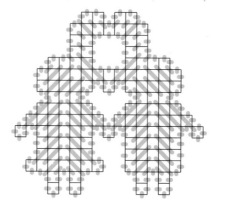

Girl Charm
(10 x 13 threads)

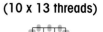
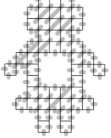

12

Jolly Gingerboy Basket

...tretched to carry lots of goodies, this whimsical gingerboy basket ...deliver a Yuletide surprise. The project is stitched on stiff ...ight size for an offering of yummy gingerbread cookies.

JOLLY GINGERBOY BASKET

Size: 6"w x 9³/₄"h x 7¹/₂"d

Supplies: Worsted weight yarn, five 10¹/₂" x 13¹/₂" sheets of clear 7 mesh stiff plastic canvas, #16 tapestry needle, and craft glue

Stitches Used: Backstitch, Cross Stitch, French Knot, Gobelin Stitch, Overcast Stitch, and Tent Stitch

Instructions: Follow charts to cut and stitch pieces. Stitch Feet through both thicknesses of plastic canvas. Repeat to make one Side A and one Side B. Match symbols to join pieces together as follows.

Using ecru yarn, join Feet to Side A between ▲'s and ■'s through four thicknesses of plastic canvas. Join Side B to Feet between ◆'s and *'s. With wrong sides together, join Gingerbread Boy Front to Back between ★'s and ✚'s. Join remaining short edges of Side A and Side B to Gingerbread Boy Front and Back through four thicknesses of plastic canvas.

Using ecru yarn, join Arm A to Side A between ▼'s through three thicknesses of plastic canvas. Join Arm B to Side between ♠'s. Join Bottom to Gingerbread Boy Front and Back, Side A, Side B, and Feet through all thicknesses of plastic canvas. Cover remaining unworked edges of Basket.

Using black yarn, join Hat Front to Brim between ✿'s and ✕'s. Using ecru yarn, cover bottom edge of Hat Back. Referring to photo for yarn color, join Hat Front to Back. Glue Hat to head.

Using ecru yarn, tack Handle to Basket. Tack Arms to Handle.

Design by Dick Martin.

COLOR	NL#		COLOR	NL#
ecru	39		red	02
gold	13		black	00

Hat Front/Back

(20 x 11 threads) (stitch 2)

Hat Brim

(20 x 6 threads)

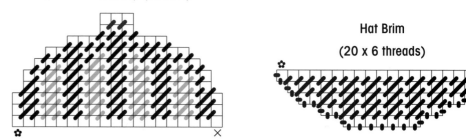

Gingerbread Boy Front (38 x 56 threads)

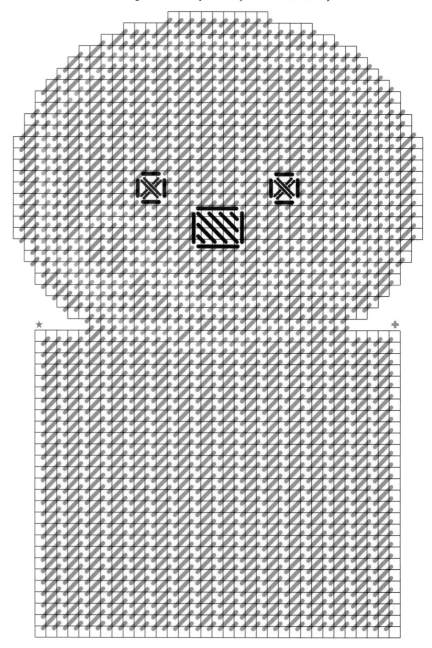

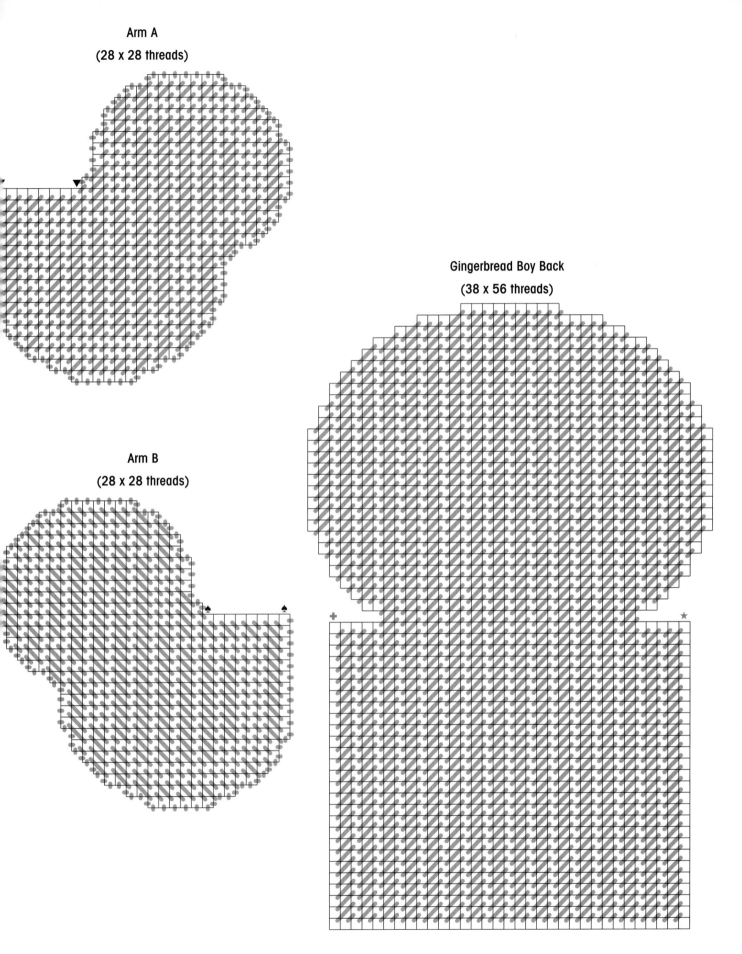

Arm A
(28 x 28 threads)

Arm B
(28 x 28 threads)

Gingerbread Boy Back
(38 x 56 threads)

Continued on page 16

COLOR		NL#
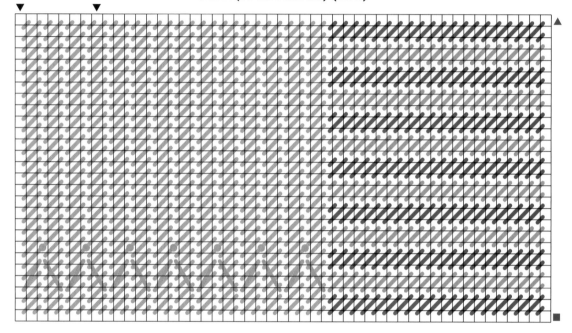	ecru	39
	gold	13
	red	02
	black	00
	ecru French Knot	39

Side A (50 x 28 threads) (cut 2)

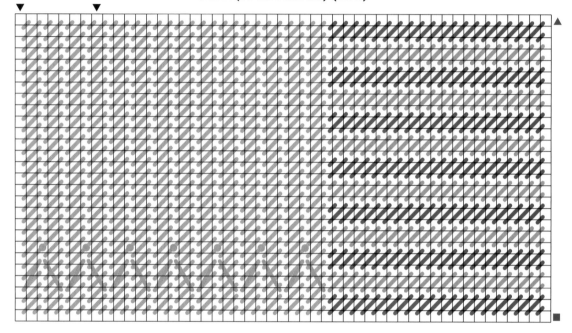

Side B (50 x 28 threads) (cut 2)

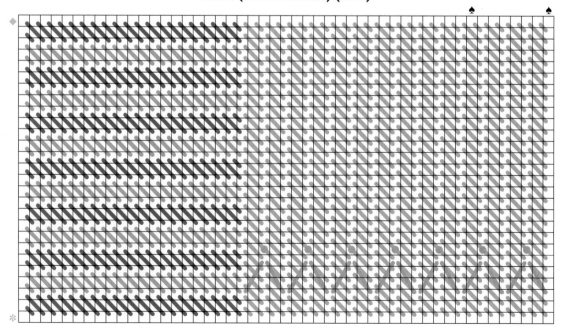

Feet
(34 x 32 threads) (cut 2)

Handle
(10 x 90 threads)

Bottom (50 x 34 threads)

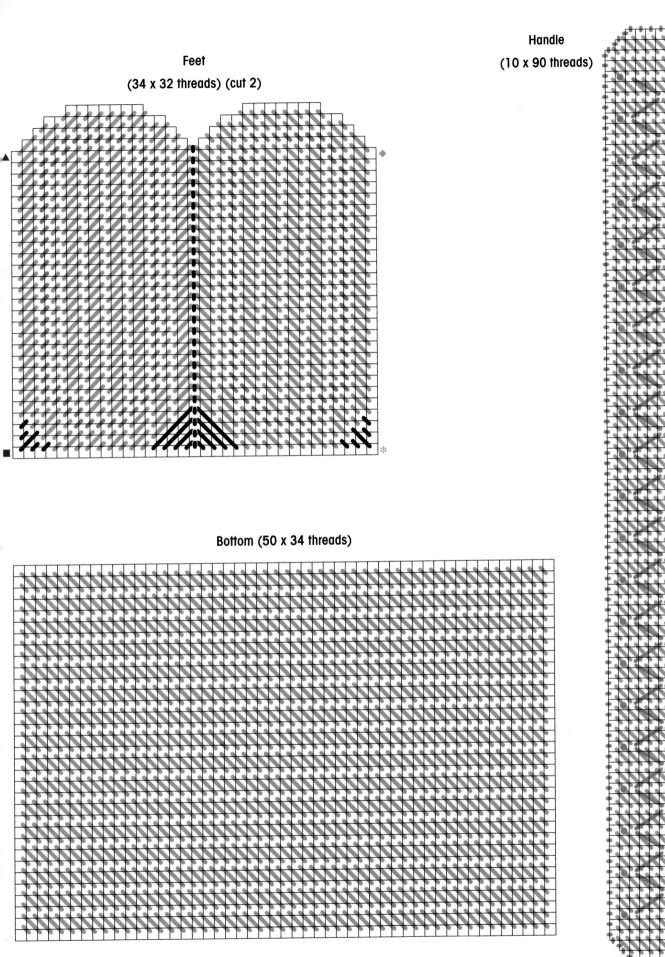

17

HOLIDAY CHAPEL

Beautiful stained-glass windows, created using variegated yarn, provide a touch of grandeur for this tissue box cover. The perfect gift for a church friend, the peaceful chapel will bring joy all year round.

HOLIDAY CHAPEL

Size: 6"w x 10¾"h x 6¼"d
(Fits a 4¼"w x 5¼"h x 4¼"d boutique tissue box.)

Supplies: Worsted weight yarn, white DMC #3 Pearl Cotton, dk brown embroidery floss, three 10½" x 13½" sheets of clear 7 mesh plastic canvas, #16 tapestry needle, 7mm clear acrylic stone, 5mm pearl bead, ½" gold liberty bell, 1" gold bugle bead, two ½" twisted gold bugle beads, Mill Hill Glass Seed Bead #02011 Victorian gold, 6" length of gold wire, and craft glue

Stitches Used: Backstitch, Encroaching Gobelin Stitch, Gobelin Stitch, Overcast Stitch, Tent Stitch, and Turkey Loop Stitch

Instructions: Follow charts to cut and stitch pieces, leaving stitches in green shaded areas unworked. Cut Turkey Loops on Shrubbery pieces and comb to separate yarn plies; trim to desired length. Match symbols to join pieces together as follows.
Using brown variegated yarn, join long edges of Front to Side pieces. Join Back to Sides.

Using green variegated yarn, join Shrubbery Section #1 to #3 between ✱'s. Join Section #1 to #5 between ★'s. Join Section #5 to #2 between ■'s. Join Section #2 to #4 between ▲'s. Matching ♥'s and ✖'s, join Shrubbery to Front, Back, and Sides along bottom edges.
Using gold yarn, join Roof pieces together along unworked edges. Tack Roof to Front and Back. Glue Roof to Sides.
Using white yarn, join Entrance Side #1 to Floor between ✿'s and ◆'s. Join Entrance Side #2 to Floor between ✧'s and ✳'s. Work green shaded stitches on Front to join Entrance Sides to Front. Using brown variegated yarn, join Entrance Floor to Front. Using gold yarn, join Entrance Roof pieces together along unworked edges. Glue Entrance Roof to Front and Entrance Sides.

Using white yarn, join Steeple Front to Steeple Sides along long edges. Join Steeple Sides to Steeple Back. Join Steeple Front to one Steeple Top piece between ♠'s. Join remaining Steeple Top pieces to Steeple Sides and Steeple Back. Join Steeple Top pieces together.
Thread gold wire through pearl bead, 1" gold bugle bead, and gold seed bead. Thread wire back down through seed bead, 1" gold bugle bead, and pearl bead. Thread loose ends of wire down through top of Steeple and around bell. Glue pearl bead to top of Steeple to secure. Glue Steeple to Roof.
Using dk brown floss, tack ½" twisted gold bugle beads to Chapel Front. Glue clear acrylic stone to Front.

Design by Bonnie Weise.

COLOR	COLOR	COLOR
╱ green variegated yarn	╱ brown variegated yarn	╱ white pearl cotton
╱ kaleidoscope variegated yarn	╱ dk brown yarn	╱ dk brown floss

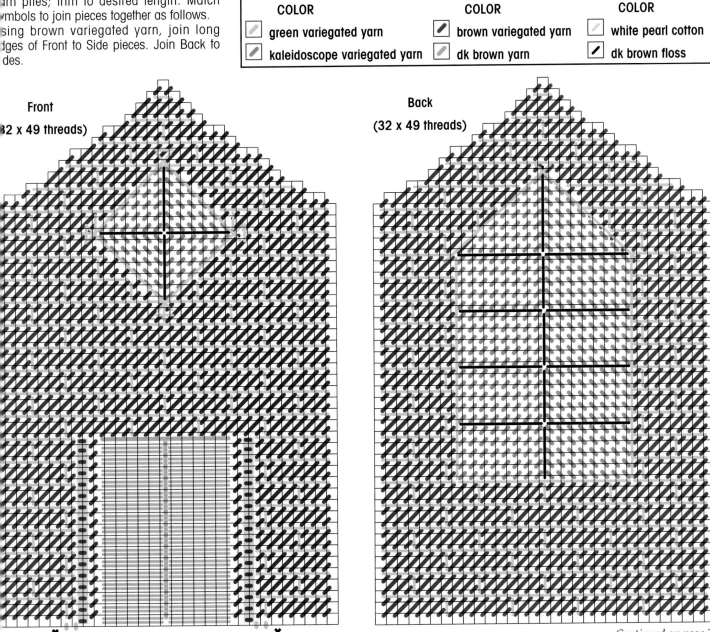

Front
(32 x 49 threads)

Back
(32 x 49 threads)

♥ ✖

Continued on page 20

Roof
(38 x 24 threads) (stitch 2)

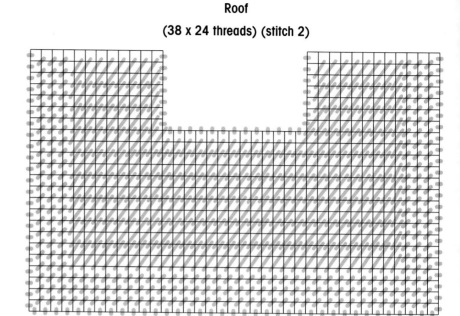

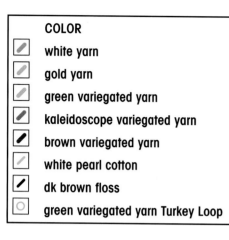

COLOR	
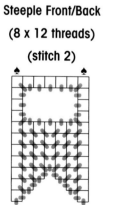	white yarn
	gold yarn
	green variegated yarn
	kaleidoscope variegated yarn
	brown variegated yarn
	white pearl cotton
	dk brown floss
	green variegated yarn Turkey Loop

Steeple Top
(8 x 7 threads)
(stitch 4)

Side
(32 x 38 threads) (stitch 2)

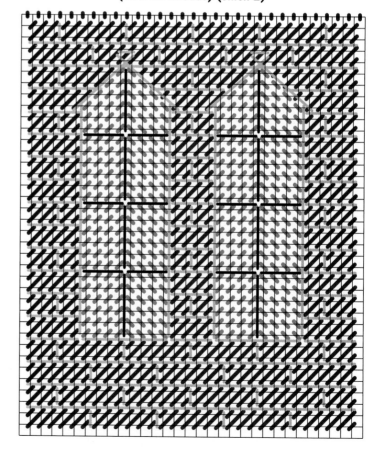

Steeple Front/Back
(8 x 12 threads)
(stitch 2)

Steeple Side
(8 x 12 threads)
(stitch 2)

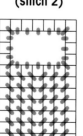

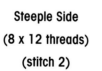

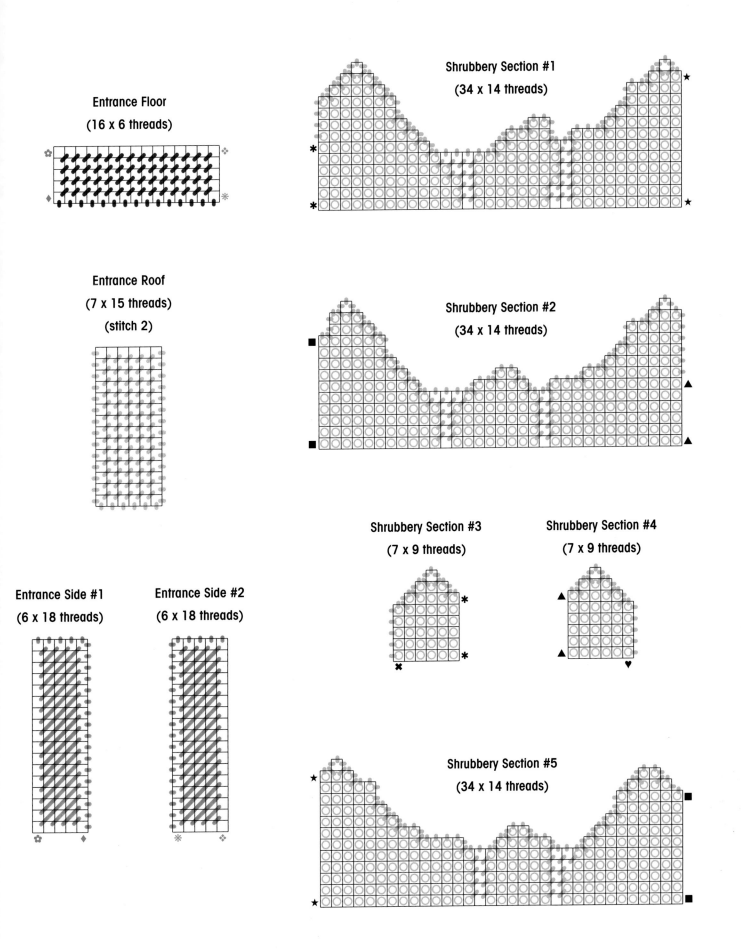

Entrance Floor

(16 x 6 threads)

Entrance Roof

(7 x 15 threads)

(stitch 2)

Entrance Side #1

(6 x 18 threads)

Entrance Side #2

(6 x 18 threads)

Shrubbery Section #1

(34 x 14 threads)

Shrubbery Section #2

(34 x 14 threads)

Shrubbery Section #3

(7 x 9 threads)

Shrubbery Section #4

(7 x 9 threads)

Shrubbery Section #5

(34 x 14 threads)

Doggie Bag

Show a little puppy love this holiday season with a gift just for dogs! Our irresistible "doggie bag" is perfect for filling with treats so that your favorite canine companion can join in your merrymaking.

hurry santa!

Special Kitty Bag

Don't forget your furry friend at Christmas! Our clever gift bag sports a frisky feline face dressed up with a dapper bow tie. Fill the whimsical bag with cat toys to include a special kitty in your holiday celebration.

DOGGIE BAG

Size: 5½"w x 13½"h x 2½"d

Supplies: Worsted weight yarn, black embroidery floss, two 10½" x 13½" sheets of white 7 mesh plastic canvas, and #16 tapestry needle

Stitches Used: Backstitch, French Knot, Gobelin Stitch, Overcast Stitch, and Tent Stitch

Instructions: Follow charts to cut and stitch pieces, working Backstitches last. Complete Background of Tote Bag Front with blue Tent Stitches as shown on chart.

Cut a 37 x 57 thread piece of plastic canvas for Back. Cut two 17 x 57 thread pieces of plastic canvas for Sides. Cut a 6 x 75 thread piece of plastic canvas for Handle. Cut a 37 x 17 thread piece of plastic canvas for Bottom. Back, Sides, Handle, and Bottom are not stitched.

Using white yarn, join Front to Sides. Join Back to Sides. Join Bottom to Front, Back, and Sides. Cover unworked edges of Sides, Handle, and Back. Tack Handle to Sides. Tack Bone to Handle.

Design by Michele Wilcox.

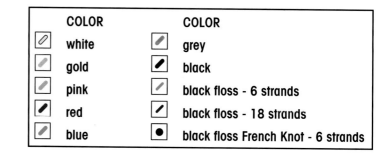

	COLOR			COLOR
⊘	white		⊘	grey
⊘	gold		●	black
⊘	pink		⊘	black floss - 6 strands
●	red		⊘	black floss - 18 strands
⊘	blue		●	black floss French Knot - 6 strands

Bone

(20 x 10 threads)

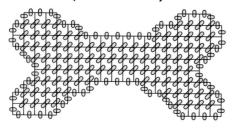

Front (37 x 57 threads)

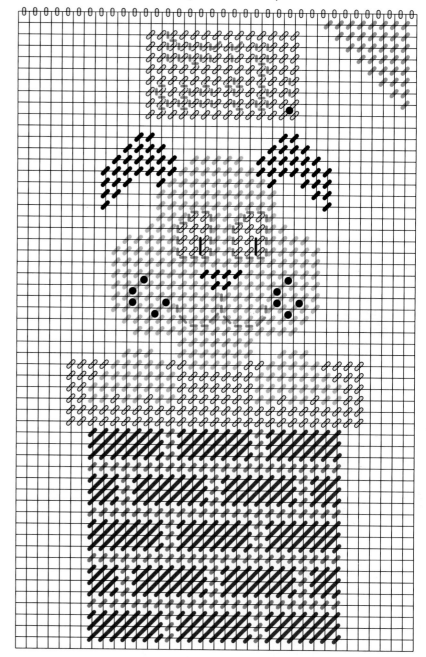

24

SPECIAL KITTY BAG

Size: 5³/₄"w x 12"h x 2"d

Supplies: Worsted weight yarn, two 10¹/₂" x 13¹/₂" sheets of almond 7 mesh plastic canvas, and #16 tapestry needle

Stitches Used: Backstitch, Cross Stitch, French Knot, Gobelin Stitch, Overcast Stitch, and Tent Stitch

Instructions: Follow chart to cut and stitch Bag Front. Before adding Backstitches, complete background of Front with tan Tent Stitches as indicated on chart.
Cut a 38 x 49 thread piece of plastic canvas for Back. Cut two 14 x 49 thread pieces of plastic canvas for Sides. Cut two 8 x 71 thread pieces of plastic canvas for Handles. Cut a 38 x 14 thread piece of plastic canvas for Bottom. Back, Sides, and Bottom are not stitched. Cover Handle pieces with tan Tent Stitches.
Using matching color yarn, join Front to Sides. Using tan yarn, join Back to Sides. Join Bottom to Front, Back, and Sides. Cover unworked edges of Sides, Back, and Handles.
Using tan yarn, tack one Handle piece to Front. Tack remaining Handle piece to Back.

Design by Peggy Astle.

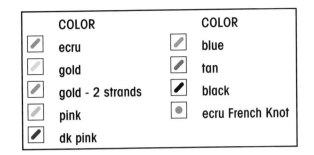

COLOR		COLOR	
✐	ecru	✐	blue
✐	gold	✐	tan
✐	gold - 2 strands	✐	black
✐	pink	●	ecru French Knot
✐	dk pink		

Front (38 x 57 threads)

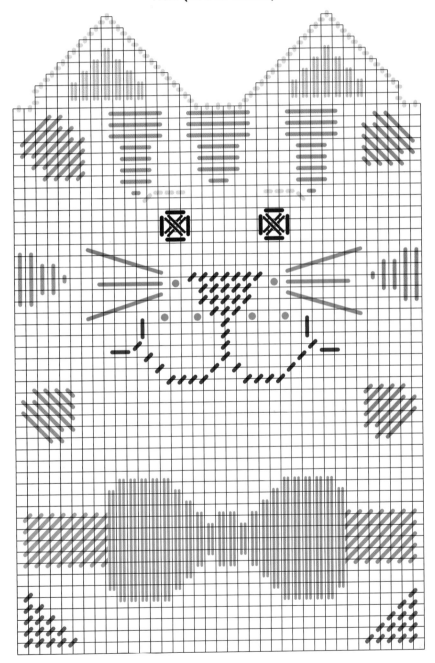

25

A+ Teacher Gifts

Teach a lesson in thoughtfulness when you present a special educator with gifts from this cute collection! A charming bag, tissue box cover, fashion pin, and magnet set coordinate for an A+ ensemble.

A⁺ TEACHER GIFTS

PIN

Size: 3¹/₂"w x 2"h

Supplies: Embroidery floss, one 10¹/₂" x 13¹/₂" sheet of clear 10 mesh plastic canvas, #20 tapestry needle, three 6mm round jump rings, pin back, and craft glue

Stitches Used: Backstitch, Overcast Stitch, and Tent Stitch

Instructions: Follow charts to cut and stitch pieces, working Backstitches last. Use six strands of floss for Tent and Overcast Stitches and two strands of floss for Backstitches. Attach Apple, "A+," and Chalkboard to Pencil with jump rings. Glue pin back to Pencil.

Design by Debbie Tabor.

MAGNETS

Approx. Size: 2¹/₂"w x 1¹/₄"h each

Supplies: Worsted weight yarn, embroidery floss, silver metallic braid, one 10¹/₂" x 13¹/₂" sheet of clear 7 mesh plastic canvas, #16 tapestry needle, magnetic strip, and craft glue

Stitches Used: Backstitch, Overcast Stitch, and Tent Stitch

Instructions: Follow charts to cut and stitch pieces, working Backstitches last. Use six strands of floss for Backstitches. Glue magnetic strip to each Magnet.

Designs by Debbie Tabor.

TISSUE BOX COVER

Size: 10"w x 3¹/₄"h x 5¹/₄"d

(Fits a 9¹/₂"w x 3¹/₄"h x 4⁵/₈"d standa tissue box.)

Supplies: Worsted weight yarn, silv metallic braid, two 10¹/₂" x 13¹/₂" sheets clear 7 mesh plastic canvas, and #1 tapestry needle

Stitches Used: Backstitch, Gobelin Stitc Overcast Stitch, and Tent Stitch

Instructions: Follow charts to cut and stitc pieces. Before working Backstitche complete background with black Te Stitches as indicated on charts. Using blac yarn, join short edges of Front to Side Join Sides to Back. Join Top to Front, Bac and Sides.

Design by Karen Woolly.

	COLOR	NL#	DMC#
	white	41	blanc
*	white		blanc
	gold	11	3827
	pink	56	758
	red	02	666
	dk red	01	321
	green	27	986
	tan	40	677
	brown	13	3826
	grey	38	646
	black	00	310
*	black		310
	silver metallic		5283

* For 7 mesh canvas, use 6 strands of floss. For 10 mesh canvas, use 2 strands of floss.

Pencil (33 x 6 threads)

Apple
(11 x 9 threads)

"A+"
(11 x 10 threads)

Chalkboard
(11 x 11 threads)

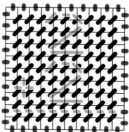

Side (35 x 22 threads) (stitch 2)

COLOR	NL#		COLOR	NL#
white	41		tan	40
yellow	57		brown	13
gold	11		grey	38
pink	56		black	00
red	02		silver metallic	
green	27			

Top (66 x 35 threads)

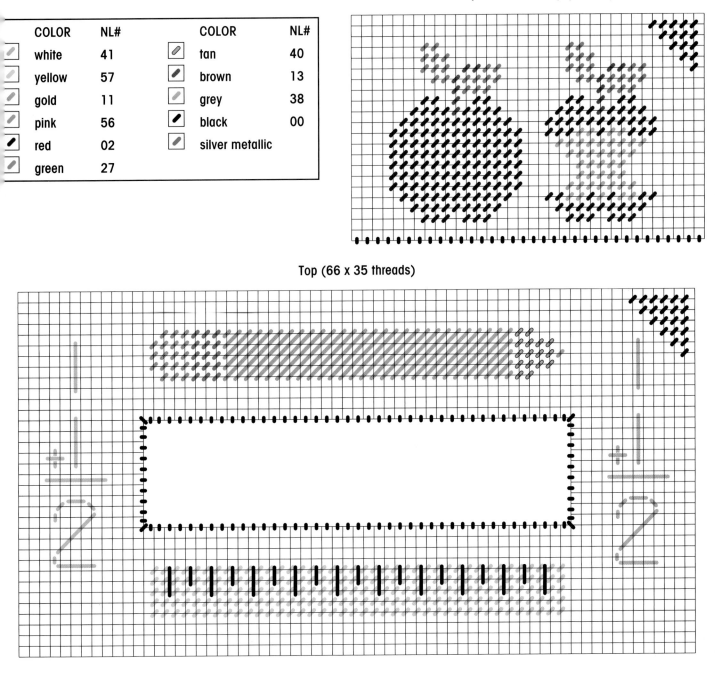

Front/Back (66 x 22 threads) (stitch 2)

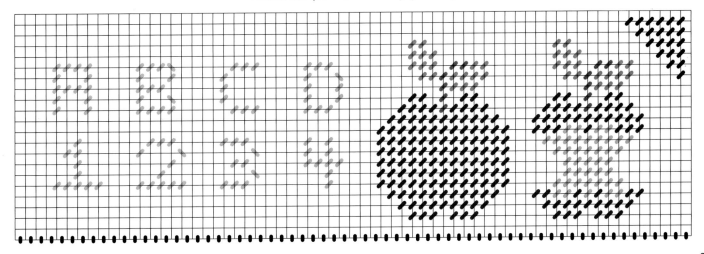

TOTE BAG

Size: 5³/₄"w x 10¹/₂"h x 2¹/₄"d

Supplies: Worsted weight yarn, silver metallic braid, two 10¹/₂" x 13¹/₂" sheets of black 7 mesh plastic canvas, #16 tapestry needle, and craft glue

Stitches Used: Gobelin Stitch, Overcast Stitch, and Tent Stitch

Instructions: Follow charts to cut and stitch pieces. Complete background of Front with black Tent Stitches as indicated on chart. Cut a 38 x 49 thread piece of plastic canvas for Back. Cut a 38 x 14 thread piece of plastic canvas for Bottom. Cut two 14 x 49 thread pieces of plastic canvas for Sides. Back, Bottom, and Sides are not stitched.

Using black yarn, join Front to Sides. Join Back to Sides. Join Bottom to Front, Back, and Sides. Cover unworked edges of Sides and Back.

Using black yarn, tack Handles to Tote Bag. Glue Leaves to Front.

Design by Peggy Astle.

	COLOR	NL#		COLOR	NL#
	white	41		tan	40
	gold	11		brown	13
	pink	56		grey	38
	red	02		black	00
	green	27		silver metallic	

Leaf
(4 x 4 threads)
(stitch 2)

Handle
(6 x 62 threads)
(stitch 2)

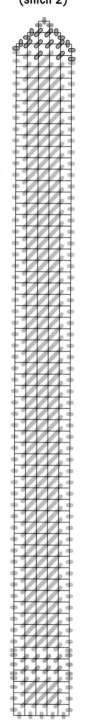

Front (38 x 49 threads)

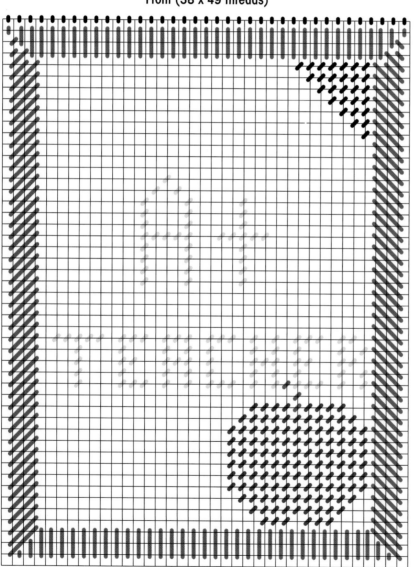

Genteel Eyeglass Case

With the classic look of an heirloom quilt, this beautiful eyeglass case will be a useful gift for a genteel friend.

ENTEEL EYEGLASS CASE

ze: 4$\frac{1}{4}$"w x 7$\frac{1}{2}$"h

pplies: Worsted weight yarn, one
0$\frac{1}{2}$" x 13$\frac{1}{2}$" sheet of clear
mesh soft plastic canvas, #16
pestry needle, felt (optional), and
aft glue (optional)

tches Used: Backstitch, Gobelin
itch, Modified Eyelet Stitch,
ercast Stitch, and Tent Stitch

structions: Follow chart to cut
d stitch pieces. If lining is
sired, cut felt slightly smaller
an stitched pieces. Glue to back
stitched pieces. Using white
rn, join Sides together along
nworked edges.

esign by Georgia A. Appenzellar.

	COLOR		COLOR		COLOR
	white		rose		green
	lt rose		lt green		

Eyeglass Case Side (50 x 29 threads) (stitch 2)

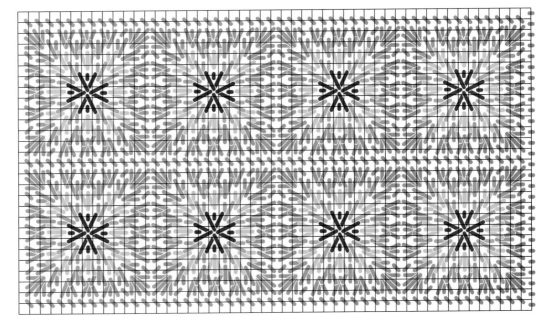

31

Distinguished Desk Set

Stitched with abstract designs in deep tones, this practical collection will add flair to his office or study. Give the pieces individually, or present them as a set — your favorite guy is sure to appreciate a distinguished gift he can really use!

DISTINGUISHED DESK SET
PENCIL CUP
Size: 4$\frac{1}{4}$"h x 3" dia.
Supplies: Worsted weight yarn, one 10$\frac{1}{2}$" x 13$\frac{1}{2}$" sheet of clear 7 mesh plastic canvas, and #16 tapestry needle
Stitches Used: Gobelin Stitch, Mosaic Stitch, Overcast Stitch, and Tent Stitch
Instructions: Follow charts to cut and stitch pieces, leaving stitches in blue shaded area unworked.
Matching ▲'s and ■'s, overlap canvas and work stitches in blue shaded area to join Side pieces together, forming a cylinder. Using gold yarn, join Bottom to Side.

NOTEPAD HOLDER
Size: 3$\frac{1}{2}$"w x 1"h x 5$\frac{1}{2}$"d
(Holds a 3"w x 5"h notepad.)
Supplies: Worsted weight yarn, one 10$\frac{1}{2}$" x 13$\frac{1}{2}$" sheet of clear 7 mesh plastic canvas, and #16 tapestry needle
Stitches Used: Gobelin Stitch, Mosaic Stitch, Overcast Stitch, and Tent Stitch
Instructions: Follow charts to cut and stitch pieces, leaving stitches in pink shaded area unworked.
Using gold yarn, join short edges of Front to Side pieces. Join Back to Sides. Join Top to Back and Sides. Cover unworked edges of Sides. Work stitches in pink shaded area to join Bottom to Front, Back, and Sides.

CALENDAR CORNER
Size: 4$\frac{1}{2}$"w x 4$\frac{1}{2}$"h
Supplies: Worsted weight yarn, o 10$\frac{1}{2}$" x 13$\frac{1}{2}$" sheet of clear 7 mesh plas canvas, and #16 tapestry needle
Stitches Used: Gobelin Stitch, Mosa Stitch, Overcast Stitch, and Tent Stitch
Instructions: Follow chart to cut and stit pieces. Calendar Corner Back pieces are r stitched.
Using gold yarn, join one Front to one Ba along unworked edges. Repeat to ma remaining Calendar Corner.

Designs by Dick Martin.

COLOR	
✎	ecru
✎	gold
✎	rust
✎	black

Pencil Cup Bottom
(20 x 20 threads)

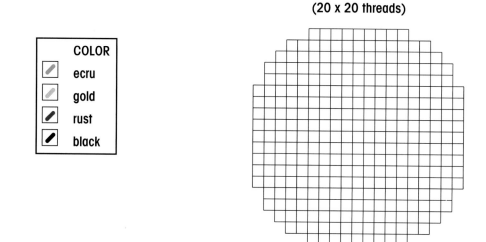

Pencil Cup Side (66 x 28 threads)

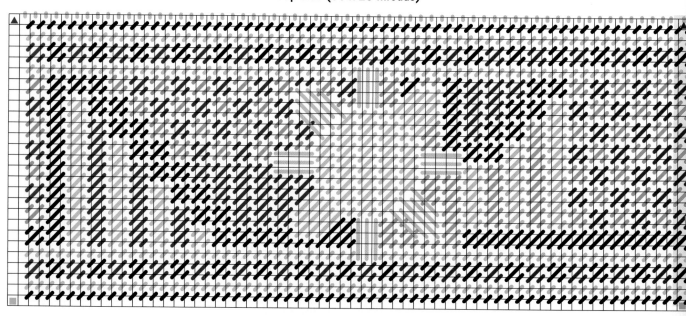

Notepad Holder Bottom
(24 x 38 threads)

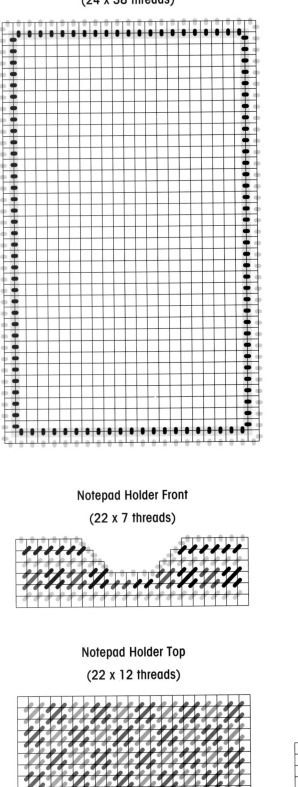

Calendar Corner Front/Back
(30 x 30 threads) (cut 4, stitch 2)

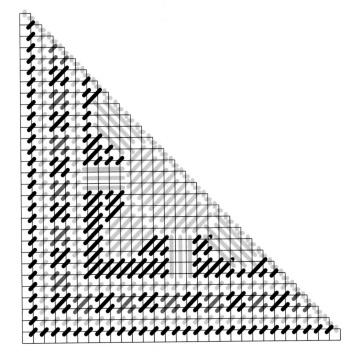

Notepad Holder Front
(22 x 7 threads)

Notepad Holder Back
(22 x 7 threads)

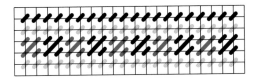

Notepad Holder Top
(22 x 12 threads)

Notepad Holder Side
(36 x 7 threads) (stitch 2)

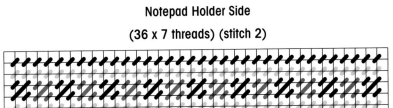

BOX

Size: 7¼"w x 2"h x 4½"d

Supplies: Worsted weight yarn, two 10½" x 13½" sheets of clear 7 mesh plastic canvas, and #16 tapestry needle

Stitches Used: Gobelin Stitch, Mosaic Stitch, Overcast Stitch, and Tent Stitch

Instructions: Follow charts to cut and stitch pieces, leaving stitches in shaded areas unworked.

Using black yarn, join Box Top Side pieces together along short edges, alternating Side #1 and Side #2 pieces to form a rectangle. Work stitches in pink shaded area to join Top Side pieces to Top.

Using black yarn, join Box Bottom Side pieces together along short edges, alternating Side #1 and Side #2 pieces to form a rectangle. Work stitches in blue shaded area to join Bottom Side pieces to Bottom.

BOOKEND COVER

Size: 5"w x 7½"h x 2½"d

Supplies: Worsted weight yarn, two 10½" x 13½" sheets of clear 7 mesh plastic canvas, #16 tapestry needle, and two 4¾"w x 5"h x 5¼"d metal bookends

Stitches Used: Gobelin Stitch, Mosaic Stitch, Overcast Stitch, and Tent Stitch

Instructions: Follow charts to cut and stitch pieces. Bookend Cover Back pieces are not stitched.

Using gold yarn, join one Bookend Cover Front to one Base between ▲'s. Matching ■'s, place Base on top of one Base Bottom. Join Base Bottom to Base along unworked edges of Base. Join remaining unworked edges of Front to Back. Repeat for remaining pieces.

Designs by Dick Martin.

Box Bottom Side #1

(12 x 28 threads) (stitch 2)

Box Bottom Side #2

(12 x 46 threads)

(stitch 2)

Box Top Side #1

(4 x 26 threads)

(stitch 2)

Box Top Side #2

(4 x 44 threads)

(stitch 2)

Box Top (30 x 48 threads)

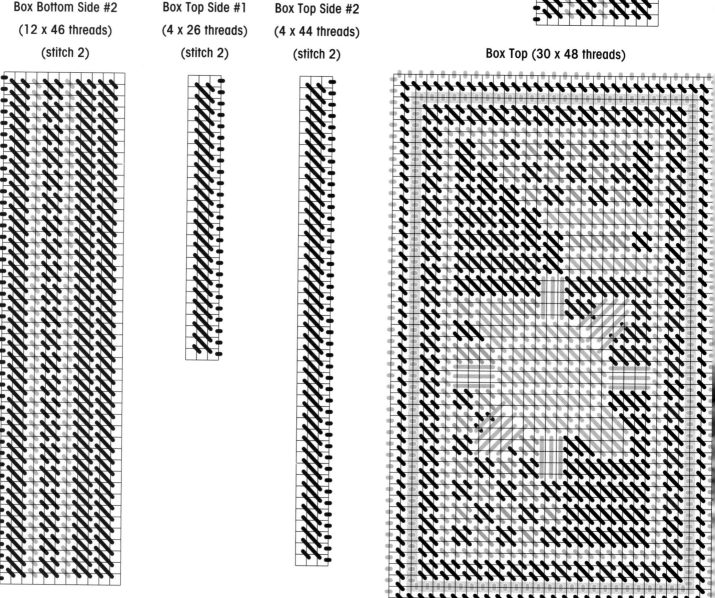

Bookend Cover Base Bottom (34 x 8 threads) (cut 2)

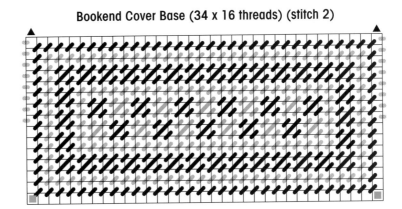

COLOR

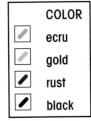

ecru
gold
rust
black

Bookend Cover Base (34 x 16 threads) (stitch 2)

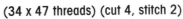

Box Bottom (30 x 48 threads)

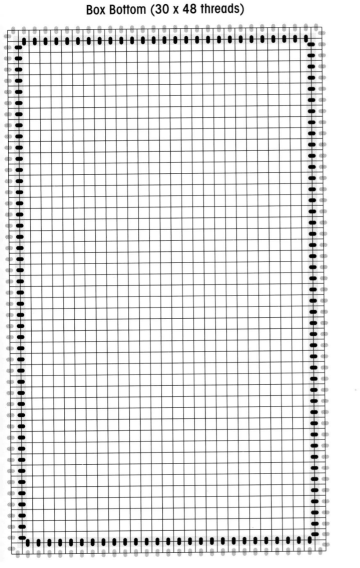

Bookend Cover Front/Back

(34 x 47 threads) (cut 4, stitch 2)

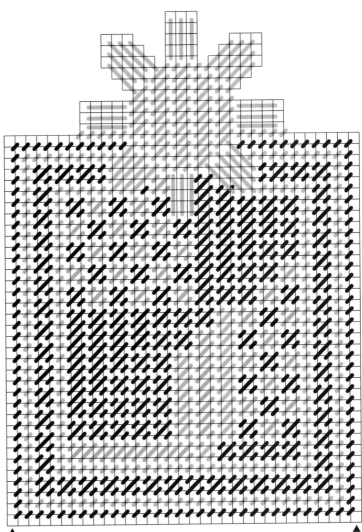

Elegant Coaster Set

Give the gift of functional elegance with a lovely coaster set. Ecru yarn and unique stitches make this set a perfect accent for any home.

ELEGANT COASTER SET

Box Size: 4"w x 2¹/₄"h x 4"d

Coaster Size: 3¹/₄"w x 3¹/₄"h

Supplies: Worsted weight yarn, two 10¹/₂" x 13¹/₂" sheets of clear 7 mesh plastic canvas, #16 tapestry needle, cork or felt (optional), and craft glue (optional)

Stitches Used: Alternating Scotch Stitch, Gobelin Stitch, Overcast Stitch, Smyrna Cross Stitch, and Tent Stitch

Instructions: Follow charts to cut and stitch pieces. Using ecru yarn, join Box Top Sides together along short edges. Join Top Sides to Top.

Join Box Sides together along short edges. Join Bottom to Box Sides.

If desired, cut a piece of cork or felt slightly smaller than each Coaster. Glue cork or felt to back of Coasters.

Design by Angela Roe.

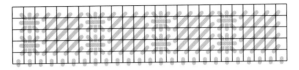

	COLOR	NL#
▨	ecru	39

Box Top Side

(26 x 6 threads) (stitch 4)

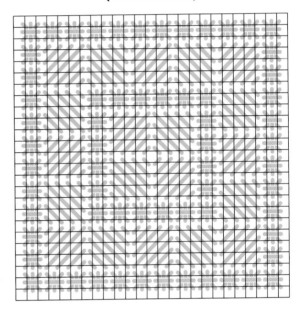

Box Top

(26 x 26 threads)

Box Side

(24 x 14 threads) (stitch 4)

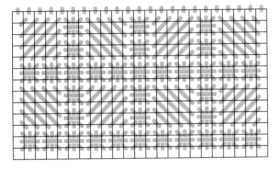

Coaster

(22 x 22 threads) (stitch 4)

Box Bottom

(24 x 24 threads)

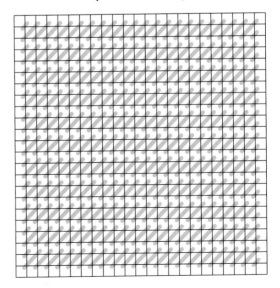

Christmas Kitty

Make baby's first Christmas extra special with gifts delivered in this adorable kitty basket! The easy-to-stitch cat hugs a woven basket that's roomy enough for lots of coordinating infant accessories.

CHRISTMAS KITTY

Kitty Size: 7"w x 5¼"h

Supplies: Worsted weight yarn, black embroidery floss, one 10½" x 13½" sheet of clear 7 mesh plastic canvas, #16 tapestry needle, sprig of artificial holly with berry, 18" length of ⅛"w ribbon, ¼" gold jingle bell, 2 yds of ⅜"w ribbon, 4"h x 8½" dia. basket, and craft glue

Stitches Used: Backstitch, Gobelin Stitch, Overcast Stitch, and Tent Stitch

Instructions: Follow chart to cut and stitch design. Use six strands of floss for Backstitch. Using white yarn, cover unworked edges of stitched piece. Wrap ⅛"w ribbon around neck and tie into a bow; trim ends. Glue bell and holly to Kitty. Glue Kitty to basket. Wrap ⅜" ribbon around basket and tie into a bow; trim ends.

Design by Pam MacIver.

Kitty (42 x 33 threads)

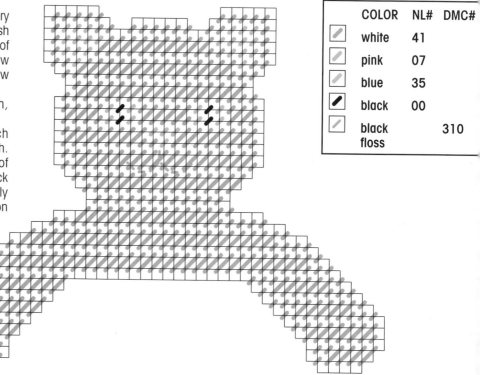

	COLOR	NL#	DMC#
	white	41	
	pink	07	
	blue	35	
	black	00	
	black floss		310

Noteworthy Bookmarks

Fancy fringed bookmarks make great quick gifts for mothers, grandmothers, and friends! The noteworthy designs are created using sport weight yarn and a variety of stitches.

NOTEWORTHY BOOKMARKS

Size: 2"w x 8"h each
Supplies: Sport weight yarn, one 10¹/₂" x 13¹/₂" sheet of white 10 mesh plastic canvas, and #20 tapestry needle
Stitches Used: Algerian Eye Stitch, Alicia Lace Stitch, Fringe Stitch, Gobelin Stitch, Mosaic Stitch, Overcast Stitch, Scotch Stitch, Smyrna Cross Stitch, and Tent Stitch
Instructions: Follow charts to cut and stitch pieces. Trim Fringe to 1¹/₄" long.

Designs by Ann Townsend.

COLOR	
	lt green
	green
○	green Fringe

Bookmark #1 (20 x 68 threads)

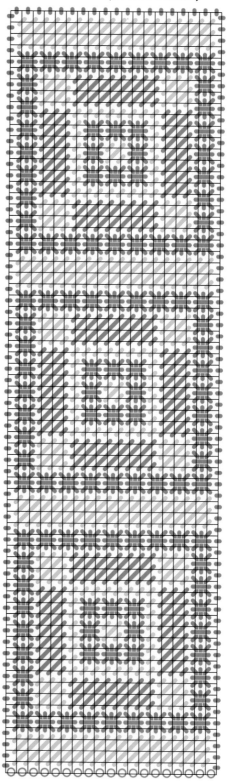

42

COLOR

⟋	lt purple
⟋	purple
○	purple Fringe

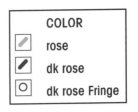

COLOR

⟋	rose
⟋	dk rose
○	dk rose Fringe

Bookmark #2 (20 x 68 threads)

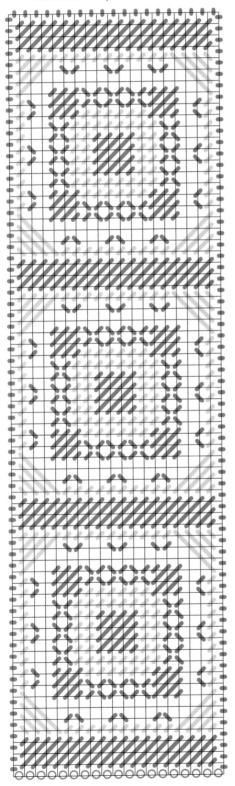

Bookmark #3 (20 x 68 threads)

Tailored Program Guide Cover

*Here's a gift idea for a television watcher on your list —
a handy cover for his program guide! A rich tweed design
adds to the masculine appeal of the jacket, and soft
canvas gives the cover flexibility.*

TAILORED PROGRAM GUIDE COVER

Size: 5½"w x 7¾"h x ¾"d
(Fits a 5"w x 7½"h x ½"d television program guide.)

Supplies: Worsted weight yarn, two 10½" x 13½" sheets of clear 7-mesh soft plastic canvas, and #16 tapestry needle

Stitches Used: Backstitch, Gobelin Stitch, Overcast Stitch, and Tent Stitch

Instructions: Follow charts to cut and stitch pieces. Using green yarn, join Front and Back to Spine with wrong sides facing inward. Matching △'s, join one Sleeve piece to Front. Join remaining Sleeve to Back. Cover unworked edges of Front, Back, and Spine.

Design by Conn Baker Gibney.

	COLOR	NL#
	gold	17
	dk gold	13
	green	29
	brown	15

Spine

(5 x 52 threads)

Front/Back (36 x 52 threads) (stitch 2)

Sleeve

(16 x 52 threads) (cut 2)

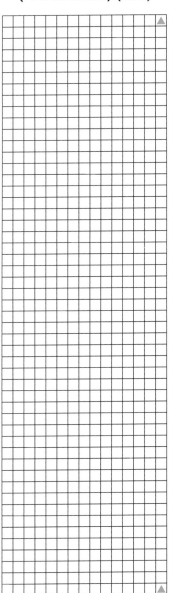

Potpourri Tree Trims

These aromatic ornaments will fill the room with the glorious scent of potpourri. Each features a cheery trim and its own design stitched separately on white canvas and attached to the front and back.

POTPOURRI TREE TRIMS

Size: 3" dia. x 1¾"d each

Supplies: Worsted weight yarn, two 10½" x 13½" sheets of white 7 mesh plastic canvas, ten 3" dia. plastic canvas circles, #16 tapestry needle, nylon line, and craft glue

Stitches Used: French Knot, Gobelin Stitch, Mosaic Stitch, Overcast Stitch, and Tent Stitch

Instructions: Follow charts to cut and stitch pieces.

Using green yarn, join one Side piece together along short edges to form a circle. Join Side to one set of Front and Back pieces. Repeat for remaining Side, Front, and Back pieces. Glue center pieces to Ornaments.

Tie nylon line into a knot 3" above one Ornament and trim ends. Repeat for remaining Ornaments.

Designs by Ann Townsend.

	COLOR	NL#
	gold	11
	red	02
	green	28
	brown	13
	gold French Knot	11
	red French Knot	02
	green French Knot	28

Side
(9 x 63 threads)
(stitch 5)

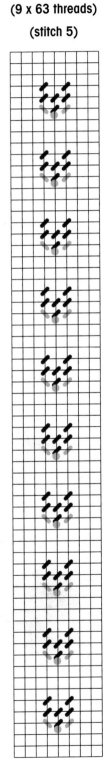

Center #1
(13 x 13 threads)
(stitch 2)

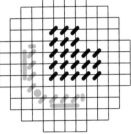

Center #2
(13 x 13 threads)
(stitch 2)

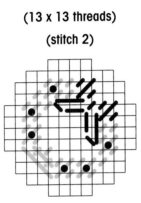

Center #3
(13 x 13 threads)
(stitch 2)

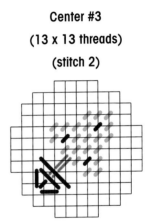

Front/Back
(stitch 10)

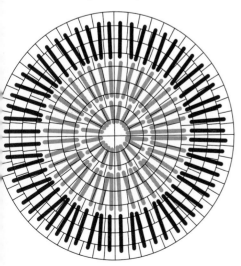

Center #4
(13 x 13 threads)
(stitch 2)

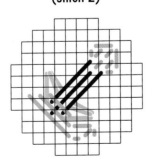

Center #5
(13 x 13 threads)
(stitch 2)

GINGERBREAD CHEER

These cheery gingerbread men look good enough to eat! The nifty hexagon box features a festive candy-look lid, and a separate package tie is great for decorating Yuletide gifts.

INGERBREAD CHEER

EXAGON BOX

ze: 5¹/₂"w x 4¹/₂"h x 5"d

upplies: Worsted weight yarn, two 0¹/₂" x 13¹/₂" sheets of clear 7 mesh astic canvas, two 5" Uniek® hexagon astic canvas pieces, #16 tapestry needle, d craft glue

titches Used: Backstitch, Cross Stitch, ench Knot, Gobelin Stitch, Overcast Stitch, d Tent Stitch

structions: Follow charts to cut and stitch eces. Bottom hexagon piece is not itched.

sing green yarn, join long edges of Box de pieces together to form a hexagon. in Bottom to Sides.

sing matching color yarn, join Box Top de pieces to Box Top, alternating Top Side 1 and Top Side #2 pieces. Using white rn, join Top Sides together.

lue Gingerbread Boy pieces to Box Sides.

ACKAGE TIE

ze: 2¹/₂"w x 3"h

upplies: Worsted weight yarn, one 0¹/₂" x 13¹/₂" sheet of clear 7 mesh astic canvas, #16 tapestry needle, and raft glue

titches Used: Backstitch, Cross Stitch, ench Knot, Overcast Stitch, and Tent titch

structions: Follow chart to cut and stitch ne Gingerbread Boy. Glue a 1" loop of esired color yarn to head of stitched piece. When wrapping package, tie bow through op on stitched piece.

Designs by MizFitz.

	COLOR	NL#
✎	white	41
✎	red	01
✎	green	27
✎	brown	13
●	black French Knot	00

Box Side
(19 x 29 threads) (stitch 6)

Box Top Side #1
(19 x 6 threads) (stitch 3)

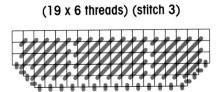

Box Top Side #2
(20 x 6 threads) (stitch 3)

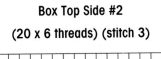

Box Top

Gingerbread Boy
(17 x 20 threads) (stitch 6)

Our First Christmas

This friendly snow couple celebrates a first Christmas together for the newlyweds on your list. Personalize the cute dangling hearts with the year and the initials of the husband and wife.

UR FIRST CHRISTMAS

Size: 7¼"w x 9"h

Supplies: Worsted weight yarn, embroidery floss, one 10½" x 13½" sheet of clear 7 mesh plastic canvas, #16 tapestry needle, two 2" sections of silver chain, one 1" section of silver chain, and nylon line

Stitches Used: Backstitch, French Knot, Overcast Stitch, and Tent Stitch

Instructions: Follow charts to cut and stitch pieces. Use six strands of floss for Backstitch and French Knots.

Using blank grid, chart initials for Large Heart pieces. Stitch initials with bottom of letters centered above dots on Large Heart chart. Repeat to stitch year on Small Heart.

Attach Large Hearts to Ornament with 2" silver chain pieces. Attach Small Heart to Ornament with 1" silver chain piece. Tie ends of nylon line into a knot 3" above Ornament and trim ends.

Design by Nova Barta.

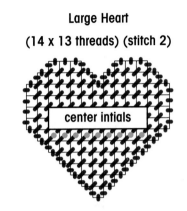

COLOR	NL#		COLOR	DMC#
white	41		white floss	blanc
red	02		black floss	310
green	27		black floss French Knot	310
black	00			

Small Heart
(12 x 11 threads)

center year

Large Heart
(14 x 13 threads) (stitch 2)

center intials

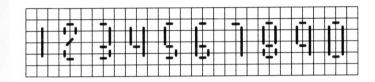

Ornament (41 x 43 threads)

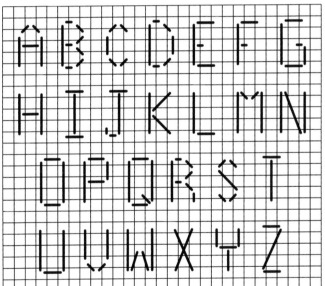

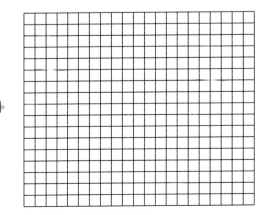

Santa Mitten

The jolly old gent is on his way to make someone's holiday even brighter! Our Santa mitten ornament, with a buttoned-up message on the reverse, will "ho ho ho" its way into a friend's heart.

SANTA MITTEN

Size: 3³/₄"w x 4¹/₂"h

Supplies: DMC #3 Pearl Cotton, desired color(s) embroidery floss, one 10¹/₂" x 13¹/₂" sheet of clear 10 mesh plastic canvas, #20 tapestry needle, four buttons (desired color and size), and 12" square of black felt

Stitches Used: Backstitch, Cross Stitch, Overcast Stitch, and Tent Stitch

Instructions: Follow chart to cut and stitch Mitten Front. Before adding Backstitches, complete background with grey Tent Stitches as indicated on chart. Thread a 12" length of red pearl cotton through one button and tie into a bow; trim ends. Tack button to Mitten Front.

Using Mitten Front as a pattern, cut felt for Mitten Back. Using long stitches, stitch three H's on Mitten Back with six strands of embroidery floss. Sew buttons to Mitten Back. Using black pearl cotton, join Mitten Front to Back. Tie black pearl cotton into a knot 3" above ornament; trim ends.

Design by Kathy Elrod.

	COLOR	DMC#		COLOR	DMC#
	white	blanc		grey	414
	flesh	754		black	310
	red	498			

Mitten Front

(39 x 46 threads)

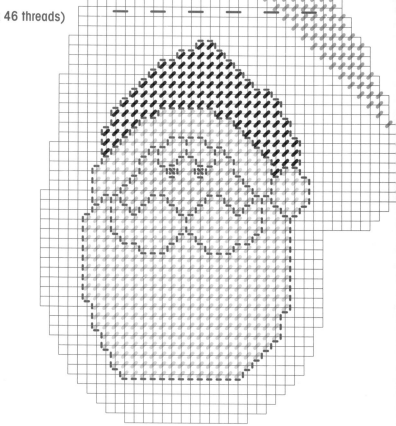

Stellar Coaster Set

Vivid yarns and striking patterns make this coaster set a truly stellar present for anyone on Santa's list! The top of the storage box features an easy-to-stitch dimensional star.

STELLAR COASTER SET

Box Size: 4³/₄"w x 4³/₄"h x 2¹/₂"d
Coaster Size: 3³/₄"w x 3³/₄"h
Supplies: Worsted weight yarn, two 10¹/₂" x 13¹/₂" sheets of clear 7 mesh plastic canvas, #16 tapestry needle, cork or felt (optional), and craft glue (optional)
Stitches Used: French Knot, Gobelin Stitch, Overcast Stitch, and Tent Stitch
Instructions: Follow charts to cut and stitch pieces, leaving stitches in shaded areas unworked.

Work stitches in pink shaded area to join long unworked edges of Box Bottom Side pieces to Bottom. Using black yarn, join Bottom Side pieces together.

Work stitches in blue shaded area to join long unworked edges of Box Top Side pieces to Top. Using black yarn, join Top Side pieces together.

Matching ▲'s and ■'s, work stitches in green shaded area to join Star pieces to Box Top through all thicknesses of plastic canvas.

If desired, cut a piece of cork or felt slightly smaller than each Coaster. Glue cork or felt to back of Coasters.

Design by Dick Martin.

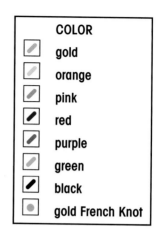

COLOR	
▱	gold
▱	orange
▱	pink
▰	red
▱	purple
▱	green
▰	black
●	gold French Knot

Coaster
(25 x 25 threads) (stitch 4)

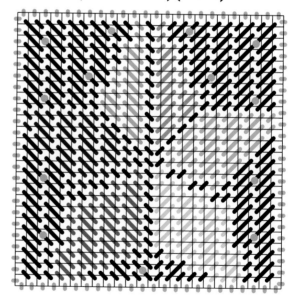

54

Box Top

(31 x 31 threads)

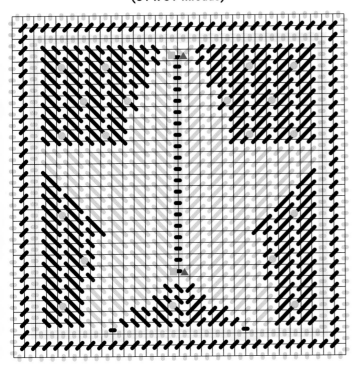

Box Top Side

(27 x 4 threads) (stitch 4)

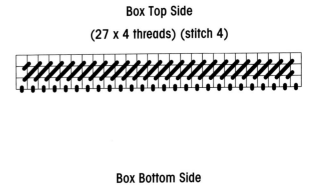

Box Bottom Side

(29 x 9 threads) (stitch 4)

Box Bottom

(31 x 31 threads)

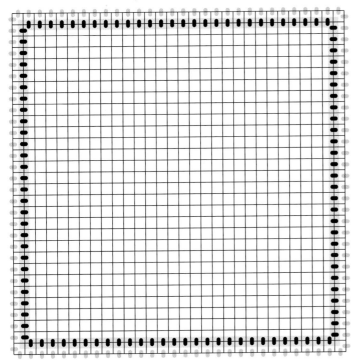

Star Side #1

(13 x 25 threads)

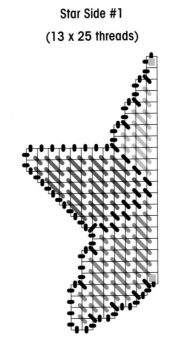

Star Side #2

(13 x 25 threads)

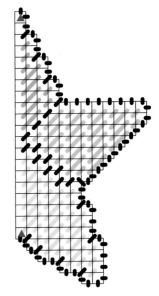

Our bright, cheery barrette holder will get any young lady organized! Fuzzy pom-poms accent the sunny face and "rays" of canvas that hold lots of hair clasps and bows.

UNNY BARRETTE HOLDER

ze: 11¹/₂"w x 16¹/₂"h

pplies: Worsted weight yarn, two 10¹/₂" x 13¹/₂"
eets of white 7 mesh plastic canvas, #16
pestry needle, thirteen ¹/₂" yellow pom poms, one
" pink pom-pom, and craft glue

itches Used: Gobelin Stitch, Smyrna Cross Stitch,
ercast Stitch, and Tent Stitch

structions: Follow charts to cut and stitch pieces,
aving stitches in pink shaded areas unworked.
r Tails, cut two pieces of plastic canvas 4 x 43
reads each and one piece of plastic canvas
x 34 threads.

ork stitches in pink shaded areas to join Tail
eces to Sunburst. Using white yarn, tack Daisy
eces to Barrette Holder. Glue pom-poms to
mpleted stitched piece.

esign by Dick Martin.

COLOR		NL#
⟋	white	41
⟋	dk yellow	57
⟋	pink	07
⟋	black	00

Daisy
(10 x 10 threads)
(cut 13)

Sunburst
(70 x 70 threads)

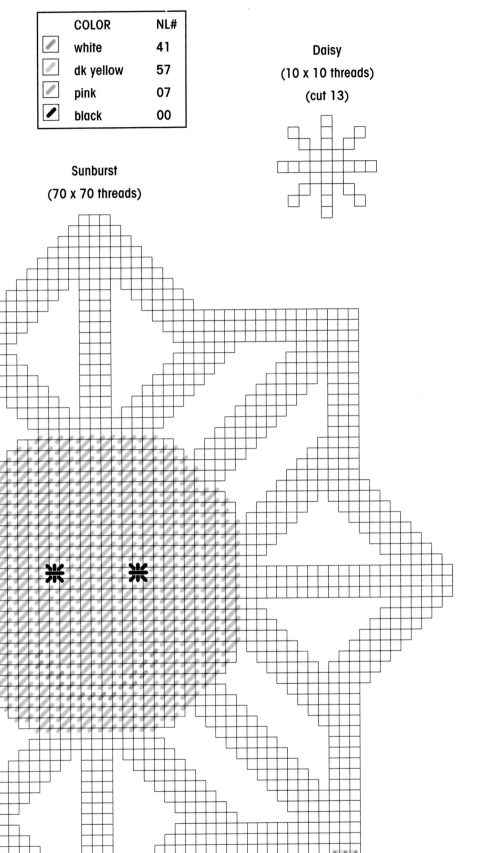

Angelic Musicians

These precious angel ornaments create a symphony of beauty! Each pastel seraph plays her own instrument, which is stitched in metallic braid. Shimmering beads add a heavenly sparkle to their robes and wings.

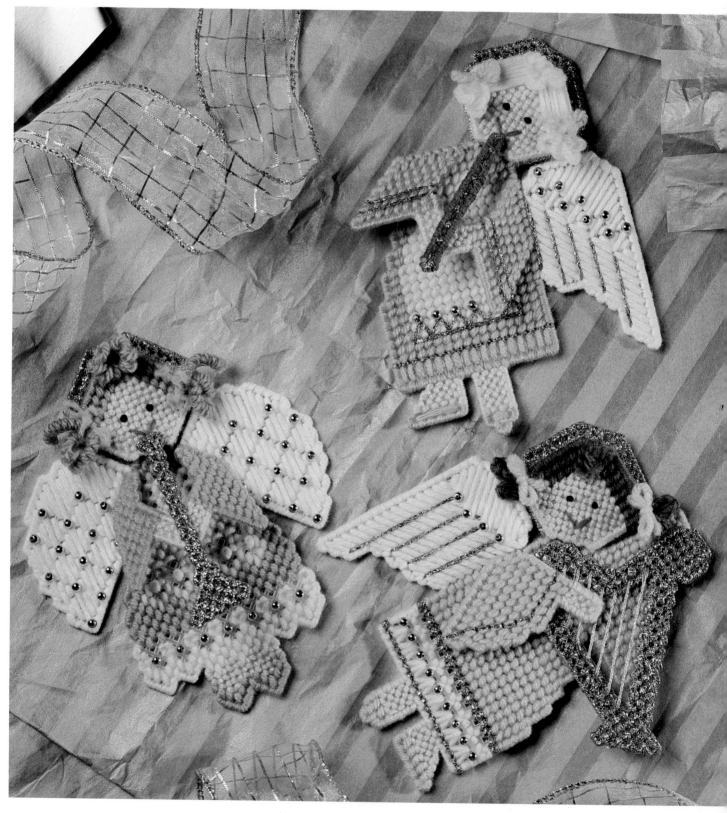

ANGELIC MUSICIANS
ANGEL WITH HARP

Size: 6¼"w x 6¼"h

Supplies: Worsted weight yarn, gold metallic braid, gold DMC Embroidery Floss 5282, one 10½" x 13½" sheet of clear 7 mesh plastic canvas, #16 tapestry needle, thirteen 4mm gold beads, nylon line, sewing needle (for working with nylon line), and craft glue

Stitches Used: Backstitch, French Knot, Gobelin Stitch, Overcast Stitch, Tent Stitch, and Turkey Loop Stitch

Instructions: Follow charts to cut and stitch pieces. Attach beads to Angel using nylon line.

For left ponytail, make a 2" braid using three lengths of brown yarn. Fold braid into two loops and glue ends to back of Face. Tie a 12" length of green yarn into a small bow around braid loops and trim ends. Repeat to make right ponytail.

Using green yarn, tack Arm to Angel. Match ▲'s and glue Face to Angel. Glue Harp to Angel.

Tie nylon line into a knot 3" above Angel and trim ends.

Design by Dick Martin.

COLOR	
▨	white
▨	yellow
▨	flesh
▨	pink
▨	dk pink 2-ply
▨	green
▨	brown
▨	gold metallic braid
▨	gold metallic floss - 6 strands
●	black 2-ply French Knot
○	brown Turkey Loop
●	bead placement

Arm
(13 x 13 threads)

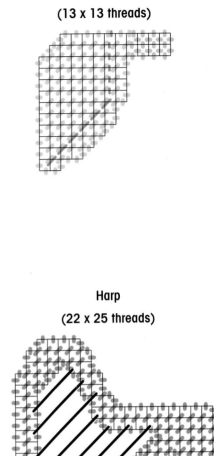

Face
(11 x 11 threads)

Harp
(22 x 25 threads)

Angel (41 x 29 threads)

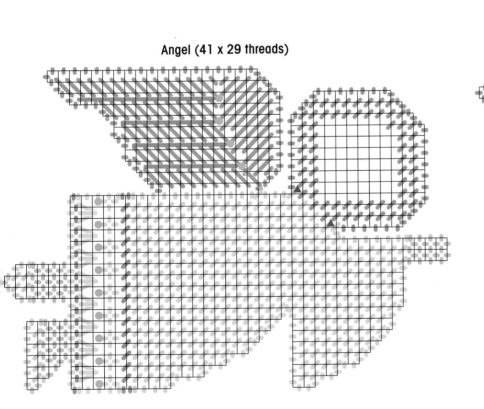

ANGEL WITH HORN

Size: 5¼"w x 6"h

Supplies: Worsted weight yarn, gold metallic braid, one 10½" x 13½" sheet of clear 7 mesh plastic canvas, #16 tapestry needle, thirty-five 4mm gold beads, nylon line, sewing needle (for working with nylon line), 12" bamboo skewer, and craft glue

Stitches Used: Alicia Lace Stitch, Backstitch, French Knot, Gobelin Stitch, Overcast Stitch, Scotch Stitch, and Tent Stitch

Instructions: Follow charts to cut and stitch pieces, leaving stitches in pink shaded areas unworked. Attach beads to Angel using nylon line.

Wrap a one yard piece of tan yarn tightly around skewer to form a coil. Run a narrow bead of glue down coiled yarn. Allow glue to dry and remove coiled yarn from skewer. Cut coiled yarn into 1" ringlet pieces. Glue three ringlets to left side of Face. Tie a 6" length of lavender yarn into a knot around left ringlets and trim ends to ½" long. Separate plies of yarn on ends. Repeat for right side of Face. Glue two ringlets to top of Face.

Matching ■'s, place Arms on top of Angel and work stitches in pink shaded areas to join Arms to Angel. Match ▲'s and glue Face to Angel. Glue Horn to Angel.

Tie nylon line into a knot 3" above Angel and trim ends.

Design by Dick Martin.

	COLOR
╱	white
╱	yellow
╱	flesh
╱	pink
╱	dk pink 2-ply
╱	lavender
╱	tan
╱	gold metallic braid
●	yellow French Knot
●	black 2-ply French Knot
●	bead placement

Face
(11 x 11 threads)

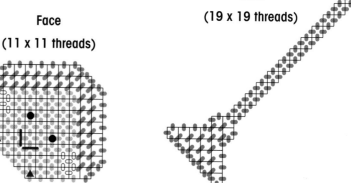

Horn
(19 x 19 threads)

Angel (34 x 34 threads)

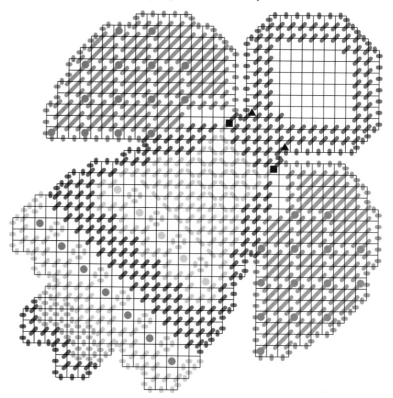

Arms

(19 x 19 threads)

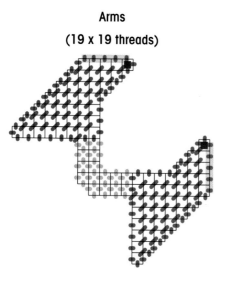

GEL WITH FLUTE

e: 5¹/₂"w x 6¹/₄"h

pplies: Worsted weight yarn, gold
etallic braid, one 10¹/₂" x 13¹/₂" sheet of
ar 7 mesh plastic canvas, #16 tapestry
edle, fifteen 4mm gold beads, nylon line,
wing needle (for working with nylon
e), and craft glue

tches Used: Backstitch, French Knot,
belin Stitch, Overcast Stitch, Tent Stitch,
d Turkey Loop Stitch

structions: Follow charts to cut and stitch
eces, leaving stitches in blue shaded
eas unworked. Attach beads to Angel
ing nylon line.

r left pigtail, tie a 12" length of pink yarn
o a small bow around Turkey Loops and
n ends. Repeat for right pigtail.

tching ■'s, place Arms on top of Angel
d work stitches in blue shaded areas to
n Arms to Angel. Match ▲'s and glue
ce to Angel. Glue Flute to Angel.

e nylon line into a knot 3" above Angel
d trim ends.

esign by Dick Martin.

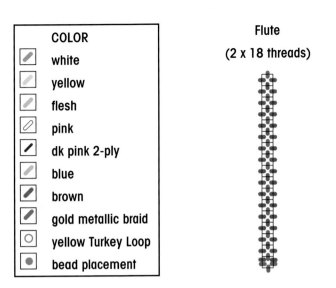

COLOR	
✎	white
✎	yellow
✎	flesh
⬙	pink
✎	dk pink 2-ply
✎	blue
✎	brown
✎	gold metallic braid
◯	yellow Turkey Loop
●	bead placement

Flute
(2 x 18 threads)

Face
(11 x 11 threads)

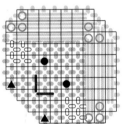

Arms
(20 x 20 threads)

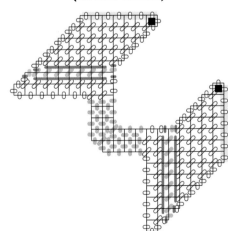

Angel (29 x 40 threads)

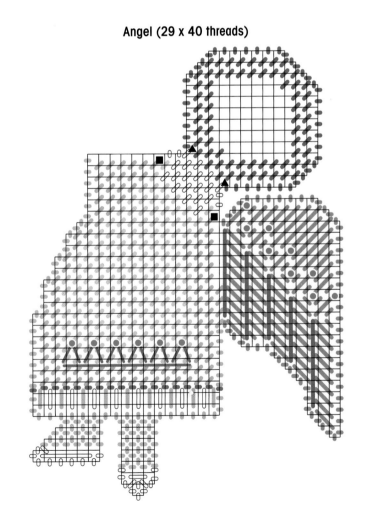

Vibrant Poinsettias

Leave a surprise for a special neighbor with this merry doorknob "basket." The flowers are formed by layering petals and leaves together, giving the vibrant piece a dimensional look.

BRANT POINSETTIAS

Size: 5"w x 7³/₄"h x 1¹/₄"d

Supplies: Worsted weight yarn, two 10¹/₂" x 13¹/₂" sheets of clear 7 mesh plastic canvas, #16 tapestry needle, potpourri, and craft glue

Stitches Used: Gobelin Stitch, Overcast Stitch, and Tent Stitch

Instructions: Follow charts to cut and stitch pieces. Back is not stitched.

Using brown yarn, join Basket Front to Back while lightly stuffing with potpourri.

Using gold yarn, join five Flower Petals to each Flower Center. Glue Flowers, Leaves, and Handle to Basket.

Design by Michael and Virginia Lamp.

COLOR	
	gold
	red
	dk red
	green
	tan
	lt brown
	brown

Basket Handle

(4 x 78 threads)

Flower Center

(3 x 3 threads)

(stitch 4)

Flower Petal

(6 x 7 threads)

(stitch 20)

Leaf

(6 x 8 threads)

(stitch 7)

Basket Front/Back

(34 x 24 threads)

(cut 2, stitch 1)

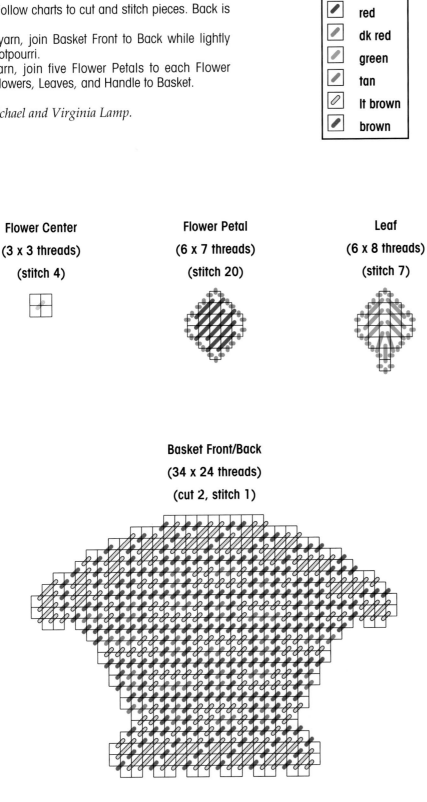

Fun & Festive Gift Set

Brightly colored yarns and simple designs give this gift set a fun and festive feel. The easy-to-make frame is ideal for holding a holiday photo, and the mug is just right for filling with cup after cup of hot cocoa.

JN AND FESTIVE GIFT SET

RAME

ze: 6"w x 8³/₄"h

*hoto opening is 3³/₄"w x 5³/₄"h.)

upplies: Worsted weight yarn, one 10¹/₂" x 13¹/₂" sheet of ear 7 mesh plastic canvas, #16 tapestry needle, w x 7"h standing acrylic frame, and craft glue

itches Used: Overcast Stitch, Scotch Stitch, and Tent Stitch

structions: Follow charts to cut and stitch Frame pieces. ue letters to Frame. Glue stitched piece to acrylic frame.

UG

ze: 3¹/₂"h x 3" dia.

upplies: Worsted weight yarn, one 10¹/₂" x 13¹/₂" sheet of ear 7 mesh plastic canvas, #16 tapestry needle, and hite Crafter's Pride® Mugs-Your-Way™

itches Used: Overcast Stitch and Tent Stitch

structions: Follow chart to cut and stitch Mug Insert. Using old yarn, join ends together to form a cylinder.

esigns by Michele Wilcox.

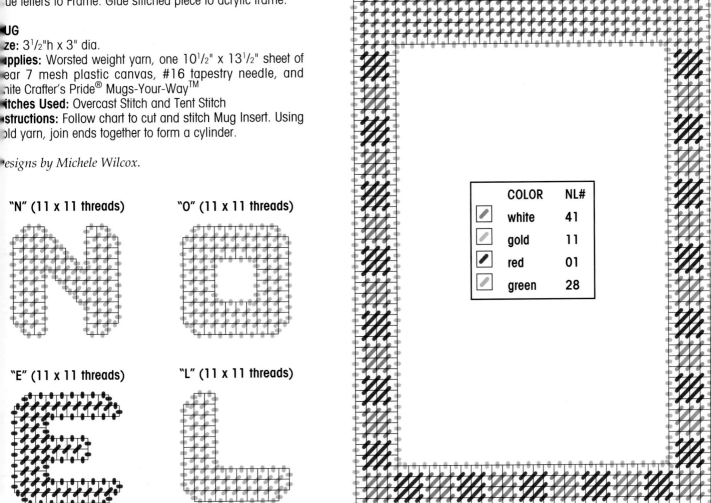

"N" (11 x 11 threads)

"O" (11 x 11 threads)

"E" (11 x 11 threads)

"L" (11 x 11 threads)

Frame (35 x 58 threads)

	COLOR	NL#
	white	41
	gold	11
	red	01
	green	28

Mug Insert (64 x 23 threads)

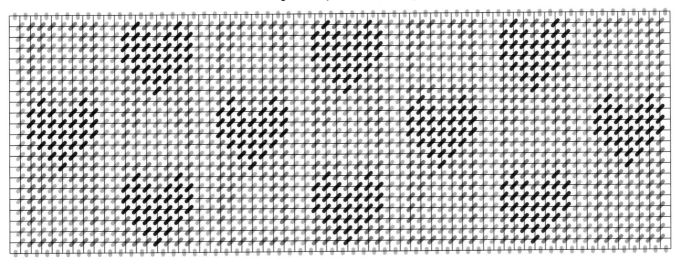

Reindeer Cheer

Instead of sailing through the sky at the head of Santa's sleigh, this reindeer team will spread Christmas cheer in your friend's kitchen. Our folksy towel holder and magnet set is a charming way to say "Happy Holidays!"

EINDEER CHEER

OWEL HOLDER

ze: 6¹/₄"w x 8¹/₂"h
upplies: Worsted weight yarn, one
0¹/₂" x 13¹/₂" sheet of clear 7 mesh
astic canvas, #16 tapestry needle, 3" dia.
old craft ring, ³/₄"w x 2³/₄"h piece of
elcro® brand fastener, sewing needle and
read, and craft glue
itches Used: Backstitch, French Knot,
obelin Stitch, Overcast Stitch, and Tent
itch
structions: Follow charts to cut and stitch
eces. Back and Hanger are not stitched.
urn Back over. Using tan yarn, match ■'s
nd ✚'s to tack Hanger to Back.
sing sewing needle and thread, tack hook
ard) Velcro® fastener on end of Hanger
at is tacked. Tack loop (soft) Velcro®
stener to opposite end of Hanger. Fold
anger, placing Velcro® pieces together.
ace ring between Front and Back.
eferring to photo for yarn color, join Front
Back. Glue Bird Wing and Beak to Towel
older.

MAGNET

Size: 4¹/₄"w x 6"h
Supplies: Worsted weight yarn, one
10¹/₂" x 13¹/₂" sheet of clear 7 mesh
plastic canvas, #16 tapestry needle,
magnetic strip, and craft glue
Stitches Used: Gobelin Stitch, Overcast
Stitch, and Tent Stitch
Instructions: Follow chart to cut and stitch
Magnet. Glue magnetic strip to stitched
piece.

Designs by MizFitz.

	COLOR	NL#
⊘	yellow	57
⊘	red	01
⊘	green	29
⊘	tan	40
⊘	brown	43
⬛	black	00
●	black French Knot	00

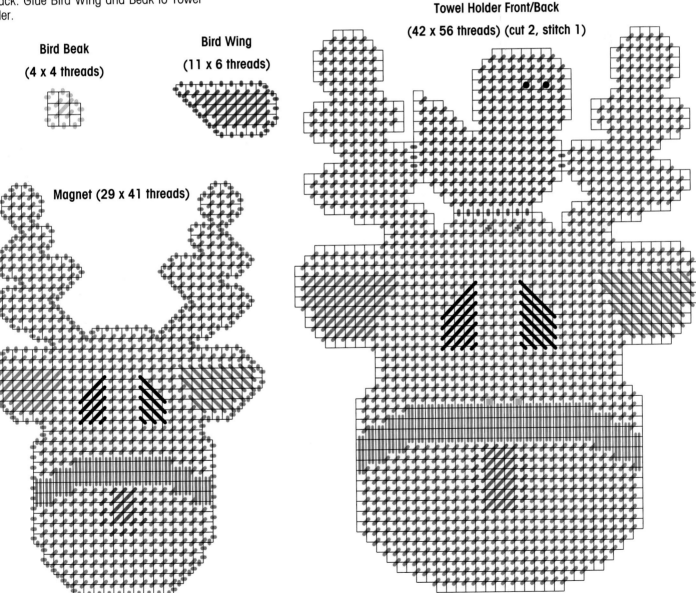

Hanger (44 x 5 threads)

Bird Beak
(4 x 4 threads)

Bird Wing
(11 x 6 threads)

Magnet (29 x 41 threads)

Towel Holder Front/Back
(42 x 56 threads) (cut 2, stitch 1)

Perfect for holding Christmas candies, these miniature baskets are cute accents for the tree. Each features three hearts stitched together with a handle forming the hanger.

ERRY MINI BASKETS

ze: 3¹/₂"w x 4"h x 3¹/₂"d each

pplies for One Ornament: Worsted weight rn, one 10¹/₂" x 13¹/₂" sheet of clear 7 mesh astic canvas, and #16 tapestry needle

tches Used: Backstitch, French Knot, Gobelin tch, Overcast Stitch, and Tent Stitch

structions: Follow charts to cut and stitch eces to make desired Ornament. Using atching color yarn, join Basket Sides together ong unworked edges. Using desired color rn, cover unworked edges of Handle. Tack andle to Basket.

esigns by Ann Townsend.

	COLOR	NL#
	white	41
	red	02
	green	28
	gold French Knot	11
	green French Knot	28

Heart Basket Side

(16 x 16 threads)

(stitch 3)

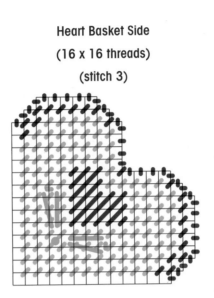

Handle

(4 x 43 threads)

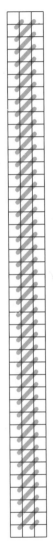

Peppermint Basket Side

(16 x 16 threads)

(stitch 3)

Poinsettia Basket Side

(16 x 16 threads)

(stitch 3)

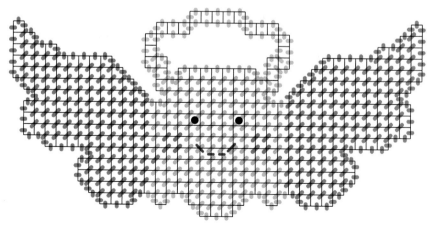

Folk-Art Angel

Add a sweet touch to a bucket of goodies with this darling angel magnet! Spanish moss hair adds folk-art style to the quick-to-stitch project.

FOLK-ART ANGEL

Size: 5³/₄"w x 3"h

Supplies: Worsted weight yarn, red embroidery floss, one 10¹/₂" x 13¹/₂" sheet of clear 7 mesh plastic canvas, #16 tapestry needle, Spanish moss, magnetic strip, and craft glue

Stitches Used: Backstitch, French Knot, Overcast Stitch, and Tent Stitch

Instructions: Follow chart to cut and stitch design. Use six strands of floss for Backstitch. Glue Spanish moss and magnetic strip to Angel.

Design by Michele Wilcox.

	COLOR	NL#		COLOR	NL#	DMC#
▨	silver	37	▨	lt blue	35	
▨	flesh	56	●	blue French Knot	32	
▨	gold	17	▨	red floss		498
▨	dk pink	55				

Angel (38 x 19 threads)

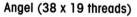

NIFTY PHOTO CUBE

Any way this handy photo cube is displayed, friends will always see a smiling face! Topped with a dimensional flower, our unique frame holds four snapshots that can be changed any time the bottom is removed.

NIFTY PHOTO CUBE

Size: 5"w x 5³/₄"h x 5"d
(Photo openings are 2³/₄"w x 2³/₄"h each.)

Supplies: Worsted weight yarn, three 10¹/₂" x 13¹/₂" sheets of clear 7 mesh plastic canvas, and #16 tapestry needle

Stitches Used: Double Cross Stitch, French Knot, Gobelin Stitch, Overcast Stitch, Scotch Stitch, and Tent Stitch

Instructions: Follow charts to cut and stitch pieces. Cut four pieces of plastic canvas 30 x 32 threads each for Bottom Side pieces. Using blue yarn, join Bottom Side pieces together along long edges to form a box. Work stitches in pink shaded area to join Bottom Sides to Bottom.
Using blue yarn, join Cube Side pieces together. Join Top to Sides. Using ecru yarn, tack Flower Center to Flower. Tack Flower to Top.

Design by Dick Martin.

	COLOR	NL#
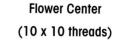	ecru	39
	gold	11
	blue	35
●	ecru French Knot	39

Flower Center
(10 x 10 threads)

Cube Bottom
(34 x 34 threads)

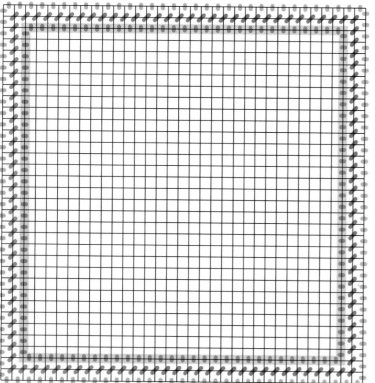

Flower
(30 x 30 threads)

Cube Top (32 x 32 threads)

Cube Side

(32 x 32 threads)

(stitch 4)

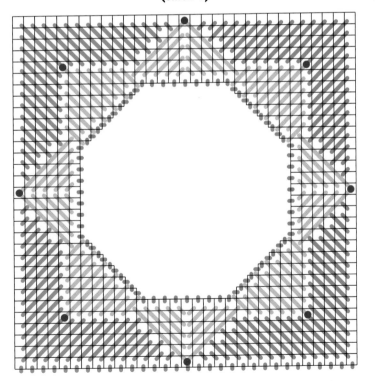

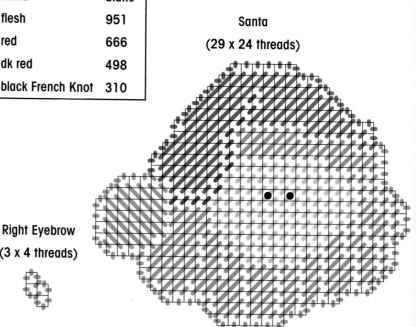

Jolly Santa Pin

This precious Santa pin is the perfect addition to a holiday wardrobe! Finished off with a tiny pink pom-pom nose, the project is stitched on 14 mesh canvas with embroidery floss. Attached eyebrows and mustache lend extra dimension to the jolly old gent.

JOLLY SANTA PIN

Size: 2"w x 1³/₄"h
Supplies: Embroidery floss, one 8" x 11" sheet of clear 14 mesh plastic canvas, #24 tapestry needle, 3mm pink pom-pom, ³/₄" pin back, and craft glue
Stitches Used: French Knot, Gobelin Stitch, Overcast Stitch, and Tent Stitch
Instructions: Follow charts to cut and stitch pieces using six strands of floss. Glue pom-pom to Santa. Glue Eyebrows and Mustache to Santa. Glue pin back to completed stitched piece.

Design by MizFitz.

	COLOR	DMC#
	white	blanc
	flesh	951
	red	666
	dk red	498
●	black French Knot	310

Santa
(29 x 24 threads)

Mustache
(10 x 4 threads)

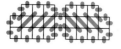

Left Eyebrow
(3 x 4 threads)

Right Eyebrow
(3 x 4 threads)

Elegant Yuletide Boxes

Gold beads and metallic thread make these miniature boxes exceptionally elegant. A dimensional tree on one box is easily created using two pieces of canvas, and a glittery bell ornament adds the final touch to the other.

ELEGANT YULETIDE BOXES
BELL BOX

Size: 3¼"w x 2"h x 3¼"d

Supplies: Worsted weight yarn, gold metallic braid, one 10½" x 13½" sheet of clear 7 mesh plastic canvas, #16 tapestry needle, 12" length of ³⁄₈"w red ribbon, six 4mm gold beads, sewing needle and thread (for working with beads), and craft glue

Stitches Used: Backstitch, Cross Stitch, French Knot, Gobelin Stitch, Overcast Stitch, Scotch Stitch, and Tent Stitch

Instructions: Follow charts to cut and stitch pieces, leaving stitches in shaded areas unworked.

Using matching color yarn, join Box Sides together along short edges. Work stitches in yellow shaded area to join Box Sides to Bottom.

Using green yarn, join Box Top Sides together along short edges. Work stitches in pink shaded area to join Box Top Sides to Top.

Tie ribbon into a bow and trim ends. Glue ribbon to Box Top. Glue Bell to Box Top.

Design by Dick Martin.

COLOR	
╱	ecru
╱	red
╱	green
╱	green 2-ply
╱	gold metallic
●	red French Knot
●	bead placement

Bell

(8 x 8 threads)

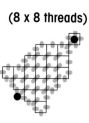

Bell Box Top Side

(18 x 4 threads) (stitch 4)

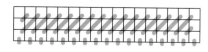

Bell Box Side

(20 x 12 threads) (stitch 4)

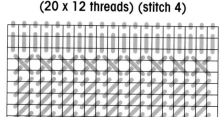

Bell Box Top

(22 x 22 threads)

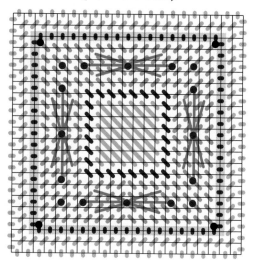

Bell Box Bottom

(22 x 22 threads)

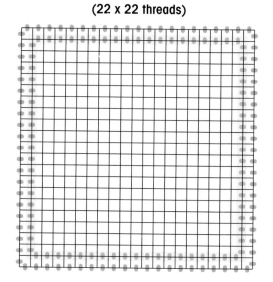

REE BOX
ze: 3¼"w x 4¼"h x 3¼"d
upplies: Worsted weight yarn, gold
etallic braid, one 10½" x 13½" sheet of
ear 7 mesh plastic canvas, #16 tapestry
eedle, seventeen 4mm gold beads, and
wing needle and thread (for working with
ads)
itches Used: Cross Stitch, Gobelin Stitch,
vercast Stitch, Scotch Stitch, and Tent
itch
structions: Follow charts to cut and stitch
eces, leaving stitches in shaded areas
worked.

Using matching color yarn, join Box Sides
together along short edges. Work stitches in
pink shaded area to join Box Sides to
Bottom.
Using ecru yarn, join Box Top Sides
together along short edges. Work stitches in
blue shaded area to join Box Top Sides to
Top.
Slide Tree Sides together as shown in photo
and tack in place using matching color
yarn. Using ecru yarn, tack Tree to Box Top.

Design by Dick Martin.

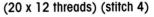

	COLOR
✎	ecru
✎	green
✎	brown
✎	gold metallic
●	bead placement

Tree Box Side
(20 x 12 threads) (stitch 4)

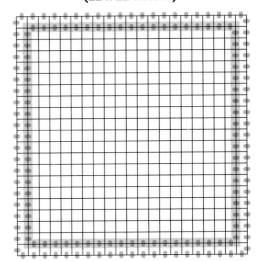

Tree Side #1
(15 x 15 threads)

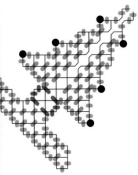

Tree Box Top Side
(18 x 4 threads) (stitch 4)

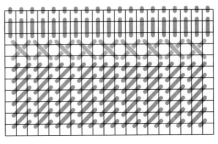

Tree Side #2
(15 x 15 threads)

Tree Box Top
(22 x 22 threads)

Tree Box Bottom
(22 x 22 threads)

Joyful Angels

Heralding angels bring thoughts of joy to any home on this striking wall hanging. Rich jewel-tone colors give the project a luxurious Christmas look.

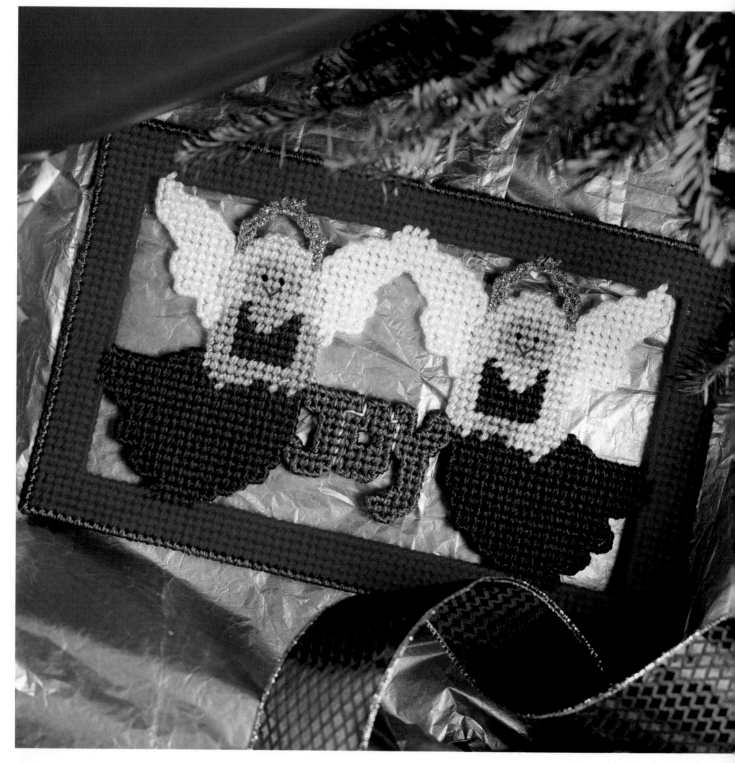

e: 11"w x 6³/₄"h

plies: Worsted weight yarn, gold
tallic braid, embroidery floss, one
/₂" x 13¹/₂" sheet of clear 7 mesh stiff
stic canvas, #16 tapestry needle,
vtooth hanger, and craft glue

ches Used: Backstitch, French Knot,
ercast Stitch, and Tent Stitch

ructions: Follow chart to cut and stitch
sign. Glue sawtooth hanger to Banner.

sign by Michele Wilcox.

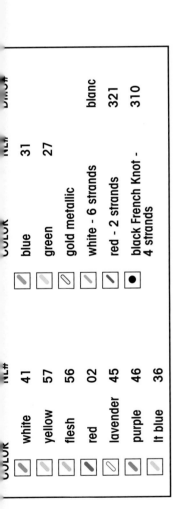

COLOR	NL#	DMC#	
white	41		
yellow	57		
flesh	56		
red	02		
lavender	45		
purple	46		
lt blue	36		
blue	31		
green	27		
gold metallic			
white - 6 strands		blanc	
red - 2 strands		321	
black French Knot - 4 strands		310	

Angel Banner (73 x 45 threads)

79

Christmas Covers

The merry motifs on these tissue box covers are sure to add zest to the holidays. Choose from the charm of striped hearts or the sophistication of poinsettias — or give them together as a cheery offering.

CHRISTMAS COVERS

Size: 4³/₄"w x 5³/₄"h x 4³/₄"d each
(Fits a 4¹/₄"w x 5¹/₄"h x 4¹/₄"d boutique tissue box.)

Supplies for One Tissue Box Cover: Worsted weight yarn, two 10¹/₂" x 13¹/₂" sheets of clear 7 mesh plastic canvas, and #16 tapestry needle

Stitches Used: Cross Stitch, French Knot, Gobelin Stitch, Mosaic Stitch, Overcast Stitch, Scotch Stitch, and Tent Stitch

Instructions: Follow charts to cut and stitch pieces. Using desired color yarn, join Sides together along long edges. Join Top to Sides.

Designs by Ann Townsend.

	COLOR	NL#
▨	white	41
▨	red	02
▨	green	27
▨	desired color	
▨	desired color	
⦿	gold French Knot	11

Top (32 x 32 threads)

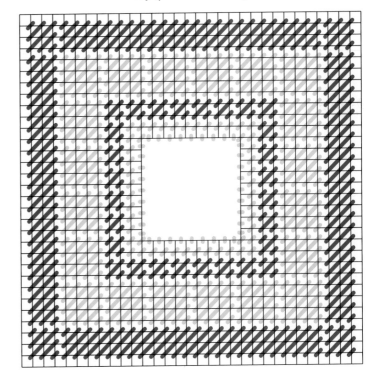

Peppermint Hearts Side
(32 x 39 threads) (stitch 4)

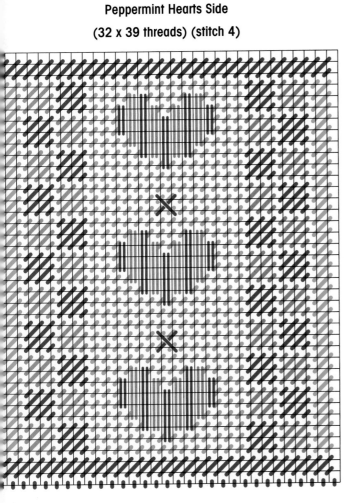

Poinsettia Side
(32 x 38 threads) (stitch 4)

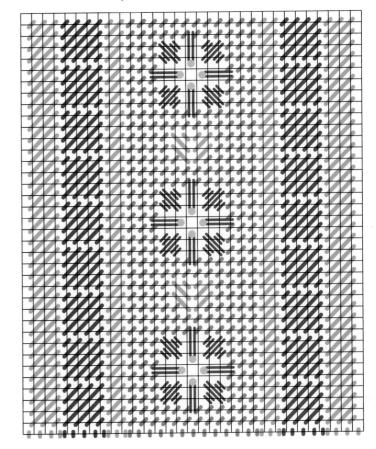

All-Star Kid

Hooray for an all-star kid! This spirited hangable features an opening for showcasing a picture of an outstanding youngster. Accented with attached hearts, stars, and buttons, this gift is great for displaying on the evergreen or the wall.

L-STAR KID

e: $7^1/_2$"w x $8^1/_2$"h

...oto opening is $1^3/_8$"w x 2"h.)

...pplies: Worsted weight yarn, one
$...^1/_2$" x $13^1/_2$" sheet of clear 7 mesh plastic
...nvas, #16 tapestry needle, 19-gauge
...er wire, two buttons or charms, and craft
...e

...tches Used: Backstitch, French Knot,
...ercast Stitch, and Tent Stitch

...tructions: Follow charts to cut and stitch
...ces. Glue buttons or charms, one Small
...r, and Hearts to Large Star.
...r hanger, wrap a 24" length of wire
...ound a pencil. Remove pencil. Gently
...tch wire. Secure ends of wire on back of
...rge Star. Glue remaining Small Star to
...re.
...ue side and bottom edges of Frame to
...rge Star. Insert photo into Frame.

...sign by MizFitz.

COLOR	NL#
white	41
yellow	57
red	01
tan	16
black	00
white French Knot	41

Small Star
(10 x 10 threads)
(stitch 2)

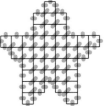

Heart
(8 x 8 threads)
(stitch 2)

Large Star
(51 x 50 threads)

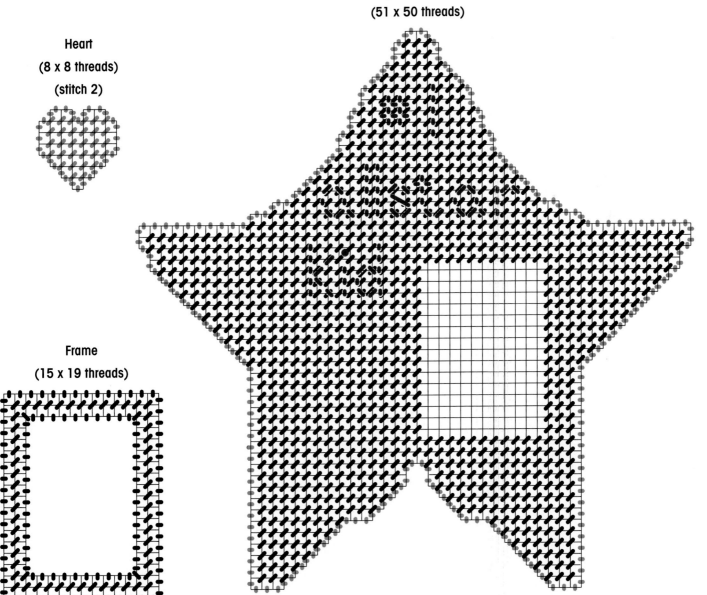

Frame
(15 x 19 threads)

83

Holiday Memories

Create a special place to hold cherished Christmas memories with an exquisite photo album cover. A great gift idea for Grandmother, the colorful cover features an attached frame for showcasing a favorite photo from the celebrated year.

HOLIDAY MEMORIES

Size: 10³/₄"w x 12"h x 2³/₄"d
(Fits a 10¹/₈"w x 11¹/₂"h photo album with 2¹/₄" spine. **Measure purchased photo album before beginning project and make adjustments to design as needed.** Photo opening is 3³/₈"w x 4¹/₄"h.)

Supplies: Worsted weight yarn, gold metallic braid, two 12" x 18" sheets of clear 7 mesh plastic canvas, #16 tapestry needle, and craft glue

Stitches Used: Backstitch, Cross Stitch, French Knot, Gobelin Stitch, Overcast Stitch, and Tent Stitch

Instructions: Follow charts to cut and stitch pieces, leaving stitches in blue shaded area unworked. Cut two pieces of plastic canvas 12 x 80 threads each for Sleeve pieces. Place Frame on top of Front and work stitches in blue shaded area to join Frame to Front. Using green yarn, join one long edge of Front and Back to Spine with wrong sides facing inward. Match corners of one Sleeve piece to ▲'s on wrong side of Front and join Sleeve to Front along unworked edges of Front. Join remaining Sleeve to Back. Glue Leaf pieces to Front.

Design by Dick Martin.

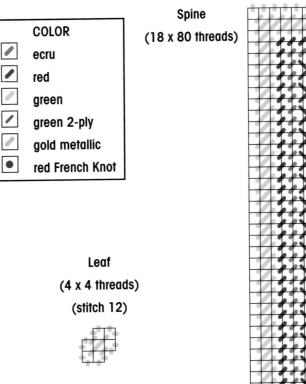

COLOR	
✎	ecru
✎	red
✎	green
✎	green 2-ply
✎	gold metallic
●	red French Knot

Spine
(18 x 80 threads)

Leaf
(4 x 4 threads)
(stitch 12)

Frame (30 x 42 threads)

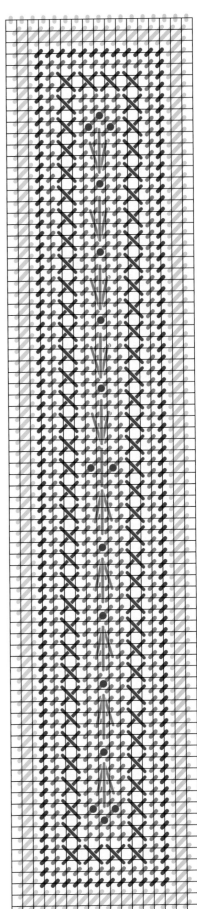

Continued on page 86

COLOR		COLOR		COLOR	
☑	ecru	☑	green	☑	gold metallic
☑	red	☑	green 2-ply	●	red French Knot

Front (72 x 80 threads)

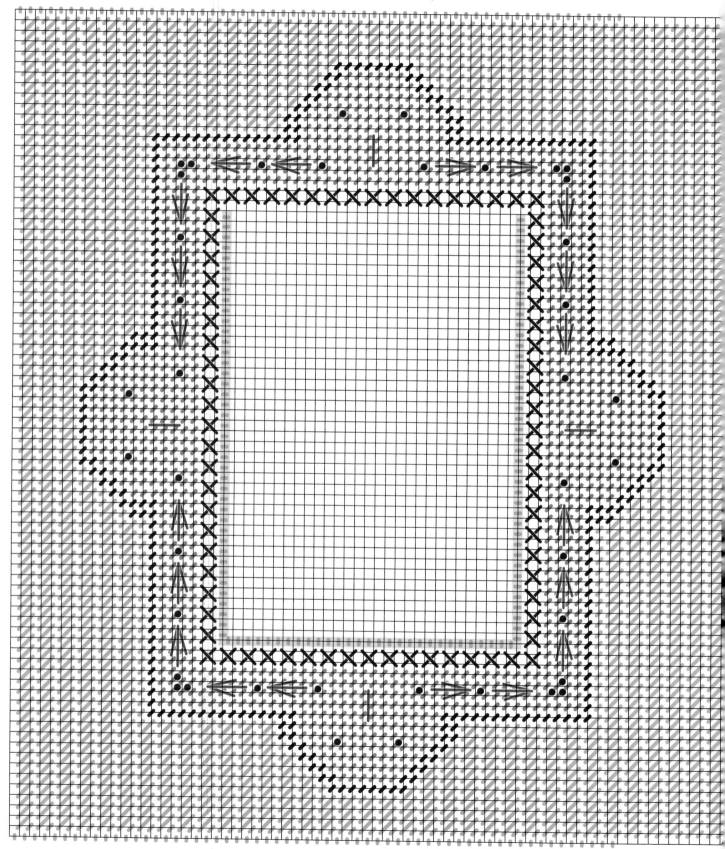

Back (72 x 80 threads)

Poinsettia Welcome

Here's a pretty holiday accent that's useful, too! Our attractive poinsettia doorstop is great for dressing up an overlooked spot while welcoming friends and family during the Christmas season.

ze: 6"w x 8"h x 2³/₄"d

pplies: Worsted weight yarn, two 10¹/₂" x 13¹/₂" sheets of clear mesh plastic canvas, #16 tapestry needle, /₂"w x 7¹/₂"h x 2¹/₈"d brick, plastic wrap, and craft glue

tches Used: Gobelin Stitch, Overcast Stitch, Scotch Stitch, and nt Stitch

structions: Follow charts to cut and stitch pieces.

sing ecru yarn, join Front to Sides along long edges. Join Back Sides. Join Top to Front, Back, and Sides.

rap brick with plastic wrap and insert brick into Doorstop. Join ottom to Front, Back, and Sides.

ue Flowerpot to Doorstop. Glue Leaves, Flower, and Flower enter pieces to Doorstop.

esign by Michele Wilcox.

	COLOR	NL#
✎	gold	11
✎	red	02
✎	dk red	01
✎	green	29
✎	rust	09

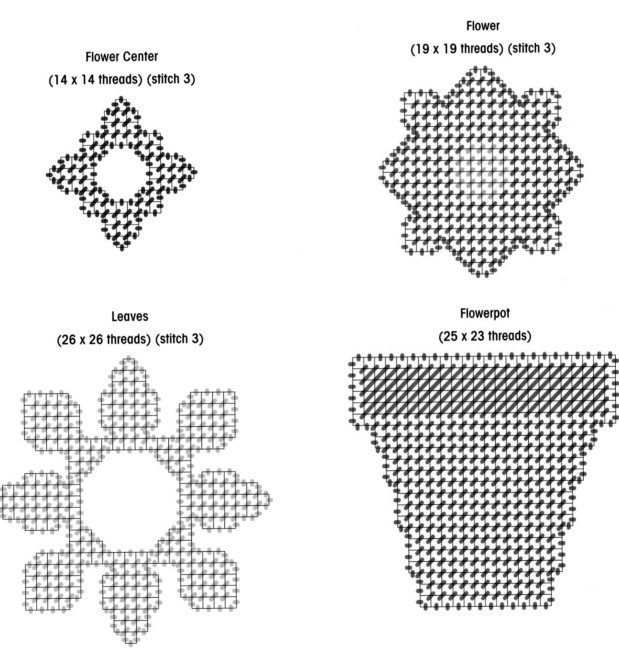

Flower Center
(14 x 14 threads) (stitch 3)

Flower
(19 x 19 threads) (stitch 3)

Leaves
(26 x 26 threads) (stitch 3)

Flowerpot
(25 x 23 threads)

Continued on page 90

Top/Bottom
(27 x 17 threads) (stitch 2)

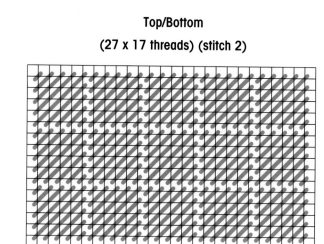

COLOR	NL#
✏ ecru	39

Front/Back
(27 x 52 threads) (stitch 2)

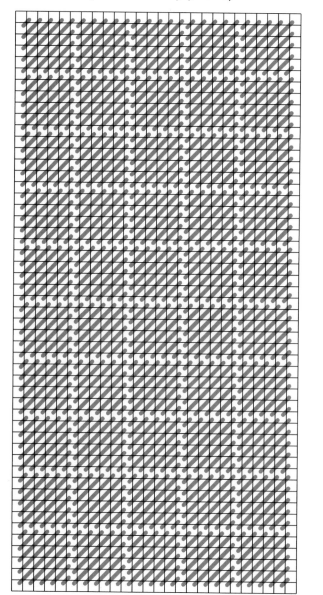

Side
(17 x 52 threads) (stitch 2)

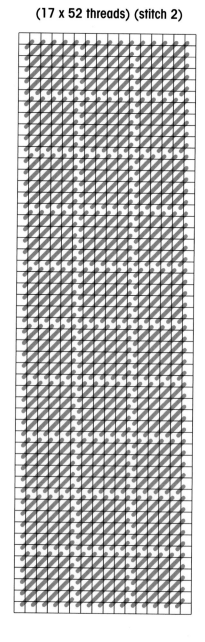

GENERAL INSTRUCTIONS

SELECTING PLASTIC CANVAS

Plastic canvas is a molded, nonwoven canvas made from clear or colored plastic. The canvas consists of "threads" and "holes." The threads aren't actually "threads" since the canvas is nonwoven, but it seems to be an accurate description of the straight lines of the canvas. The holes, as you would expect, are the spaces between the threads. The threads are often referred to in the project instructions, especially when cutting out plastic canvas pieces. The instructions for stitches will always refer to holes when explaining where to place your needle to make a stitch.

Types of Canvas. The main difference between types of plastic canvas is the mesh size. Mesh size refers to the number of holes in one inch of canvas. The most common mesh sizes are 5 mesh, 7 mesh, 10 mesh, and 14 mesh. Five mesh means that there are 5 holes in every inch of canvas. Likewise, there are 7 holes in every inch of 7 mesh canvas, 10 holes in every inch of 10 mesh canvas, and 14 holes in every inch of 14 mesh canvas. Seven mesh canvas is the most popular size for the majority of projects.

Your project supply list will tell you what size mesh you need to buy. Be sure to use the mesh size the project instructions recommend. If your project calls for 7 mesh canvas and you use 10 mesh, your finished project will be much smaller than expected. For example, suppose your instructions tell you to use 7 mesh canvas to make a boutique tissue box cover. You will need to cut each side 30 x 38 threads so they will measure $4^{1}/_{2}$" x $5^{3}/_{4}$" each. But if you were using 10 mesh canvas your sides would only measure 3" x $3^{7}/_{8}$"! Needless to say, your tissue box cover from 10 mesh canvas would not fit a boutique tissue box.

Most plastic canvas is made from clear plastic, but colored canvas is also available. Colored plastic is ideal when you don't want to stitch the entire background.

When buying canvas, you may find that some canvas is firm and rigid, while other canvas is softer and more pliable. To decide which type of canvas is right for your project, think of how the project will be used. If you are making a box or container, you will want to use firmer canvas so that the box will be sturdy and not buckle after handling. If you are making a tissue box cover, you will not need the firmer canvas because the tissue box will support the canvas and prevent warping. Softer canvas is better for projects that require a piece of canvas to be bent before it is joined to another piece.

Amount of Canvas. The project supply list usually tells you how much canvas you will need to complete the project. When buying your canvas, remember that several different manufacturers produce plastic canvas. Therefore, there are often slight variations in canvas, such as different thicknesses of threads or a small difference in mesh size. Because of these variations, try to buy enough canvas for your entire project at the same time and place. As a general rule, it is always better to buy too much canvas and have leftovers than to run out of canvas before you finish your project. By buying a little extra canvas, you not only allow for mistakes, but have extra canvas for practicing your stitches. Scraps of canvas are also excellent for making magnets and other small projects.

SELECTING YARN

You're probably thinking, "How do I select my yarn from the thousands of choices available?" Well, we have a few hints to help you choose the perfect yarns for your project and your budget.

Yarn Weight. We used various brands of worsted weight yarn to stitch some of the photography models for this book. You may wish to use Needloft® Plastic Canvas Yarn in place of the worsted weight yarn. To help you select colors for your projects, we have included numbers for Needloft yarn in some of our color keys. Needloft yarn is suitable only for 7 mesh plastic canvas. Refer to Types of Yarn, page 92, for additional information.

Yarn Cost. Cost may also be a factor in your yarn selection. Again, acrylic yarn is a favorite because it is reasonably priced and comes in a wide variety of colors. However, if your project is something extra special, you may want to spend a little more on tapestry yarn or Persian wool yarn to get certain shades of color.

Dye Lot Variations. It is important to buy all of the yarn you need to complete your project from the same dye lot. Although variations in color may be slight when yarns from two different dye lots are held together, the variation is usually apparent on a stitched piece.

Embroidery Floss. Embroidery floss consists of six strands that are twisted together. To ensure smoother stitches, separate the strands of floss and realign them before threading your needle. Refer to the color key or project instructions for the number of strands to use for each project.

Yarn Colors. Choosing colors can be fun, but sometimes a little difficult. Your project will tell you what yarn colors you will need. When you begin searching for the recommended colors, you may be slightly overwhelmed by the different shades of each color. Here are a few guidelines to consider when choosing your colors.

Consider where you are going to place the finished project. If the project is going in a particular room in your house, match your yarn to the room's colors.

Try not to mix very bright colors with dull colors. For example, if you're stitching a project using country colors, don't use a bright Christmas red with country blues and greens. Instead, use a maroon or country red. Likewise, if you are stitching a bright tissue box cover for a child's room, don't use country blue with bright red, yellow, and green.

Some projects require several shades of a color, such as shades of pink for a flower. Be sure your shades blend well together.

Sometimes, you may have trouble finding three or four shades of a color. If you think your project warrants the extra expense, you can usually find several shades of a color available in tapestry yarn or Persian wool yarn.

Remember, you don't have to use the colors suggested in the color key. If you find a red tissue box cover that you really like, but your house is decorated in blue, change the colors in the tissue box cover to blue!

Yarn Yardage Estimator. A handy way of estimating yardage is to make a yarn yardage estimator. Cut a one-yard piece of yarn for each different stitch used in your project. For each stitch, work as many stitches as you can with the one-yard length of yarn.

To use your yarn yardage estimator, count the number of stitches you were able to make, suppose 72 Tent Stitches. Now look at the chart for the project you want to make. Estimate the number of ecru Tent Stitches on the chart, suppose 150. Now divide the estimated number of ecru stitches by the actual number stitched with a yard of yarn. One hundred fifty divided by 72 is approximately two. So you will need about two yards of ecru yarn to make your project. Repeat this for all stitches and yarn colors. To allow for repairs and practice

Continued on page 92

stitches, purchase extra yardage of each color. If you have yarn left over, remember that scraps of yarn are perfect for small projects such as magnets or when you need just a few inches of a particular color for another project.

TYPES OF YARN

Yarn Usage. The first question to ask when choosing yarn is, "How will my project be used?" If your finished project will be handled or used a lot, such as a coaster or magnet, you will want to use a durable, washable yarn. We highly recommend acrylic or nylon yarn for plastic canvas. It can be washed repeatedly and holds up well to frequent usage and handling. If your finished project won't be handled or used frequently, such as a framed picture or a bookend, you are not limited to washable yarns.

The types of yarns available are endless, and each grouping of yarn has its own characteristics and uses. The following is a brief description of some common yarns used for plastic canvas.

Worsted Weight Yarn. This yarn may be found in acrylic, wool, wool blends, and a variety of other fiber contents. Worsted weight yarn is the most popular yarn used for 7 mesh plastic canvas because one strand covers the canvas very well. This yarn is inexpensive and comes in a wide range of colors.

Most brands of worsted weight yarn have four plies that are twisted together to form one strand. When the color key indicates "2-ply," separate the strand of yarn and stitch using only two of the four plies.

Needloft® Yarn will not easily separate. When the instructions call for "2-ply" yarn, we recommend that you substitute with six strands of embroidery floss.

Sport Weight Yarn. This yarn has four thin plies that are twisted together to form one strand. Like worsted weight yarn, sport weight yarn comes in a variety of fiber contents. The color selection in sport weight yarn is more limited than in other types of yarns. You may want to use a double strand of sport weight yarn for better coverage of your 7 mesh canvas. Sport weight yarn works nicely for 10 mesh canvas.

Tapestry Yarn. This is a thin wool yarn. Because tapestry yarn is available in a wider variety of colors than other yarns, it may be used when several shades of the same color are desired. For example, if you need five shades of pink to stitch a flower, you may choose tapestry yarn for a better blending of colors. Tapestry yarn is ideal for working on 10 mesh canvas. However, it is a more expensive yarn and requires two strands to cover 7 mesh canvas. Projects made with tapestry yarn cannot be washed.

Persian Wool. This is a wool yarn that is made up of three loosely twisted plies. The plies should be separated and realigned before you thread your needle. Like tapestry yarn, Persian yarn has more shades of each color from which to choose. It also has a nap similar to the nap of velvet. To determine the direction of the nap, run the yarn through your fingers. When you rub "with the nap," the yarn feels smooth; but when you rub "against the nap," the yarn feels rough. For smoother and prettier stitches on your project, stitching should be done "with the nap." The yarn fibers will stand out when stitching is done "against the nap." Because of the wool content, you cannot wash projects made with Persian yarn.

Pearl Cotton. Sometimes #3 pearl cotton is used on plastic canvas to give it a dressy, lacy look. It is not meant to cover 7 mesh canvas completely but to enhance it. Pearl cotton works well on 10 mesh canvas when you want your needlework to have a satiny sheen. If you cannot locate #3 pearl cotton in your area, you can substitute with 12 strands of embroidery floss.

SELECTING NEEDLES

Stitching on plastic canvas should be done with a blunt needle called a tapestry needle. Tapestry needles are sized by numbers; the higher the number, the smaller the needle. The correct size needle to use depends on the canvas mesh size and the yarn thickness. The needle should be small enough to allow the threaded needle to pass through the canvas holes easily, without disturbing canvas threads. The eye of the needle should be large enough to allow yarn to be threaded easily. If the eye is too small, the yarn will wear thin and may break. You will find the recommended needle size listed in the supply section of each project.

WORKING WITH PLASTIC CANVAS

Throughout this book, the lines of t canvas will be referred to as thread However, they are not actually "thread since the canvas is nonwoven. To c plastic canvas pieces accurately, cou **threads** (not **holes**) as shown in **Fig. 1**.

Fig. 1

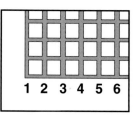

Thread Count. Before cutting your piece notice the thread count of each piece o your chart. The thread count is usual located above the piece on the chart. Th thread count tells you the number of threac in the width and the height of the canvc piece. Follow the thread count to cut out rectangle the specified size. Remember count **threads**, not **holes**. If you accidenta count holes, your piece is going to be th wrong size. Follow the chart to trim th rectangle into the desired shape.

Marking the Canvas. If you find necessary to mark on the canvas, use c overhead projector pen. Outline shape wi" pen, cut out shape, and remove marking with a damp paper towel.

Cutting the Canvas. A good pair c household scissors is recommended fc cutting plastic canvas. However, a cro knife is helpful when cutting a small are from the center of a larger piece of canva: For example, a craft knife is recommende for cutting the opening out of a tissue bc cover top. When using a craft knife, be su to protect the table below your canvas. layer of cardboard or a magazine shoul provide enough padding to protect you table.

When cutting canvas, be sure to cut a close to the thread as possible withou cutting into the thread. If you don't cut clos enough, "nubs" or "pickets" will be left o the edge of your canvas. Be sure to cut a nubs from the canvas before you begin t stitch, because nubs will snag the yarn an are difficult to cover.

hen cutting plastic canvas along a
agonal, cut through the center of each
tersection. This will leave enough plastic
nvas on both sides of the cut so that
th pieces of canvas may be used.
agonal corners will also snag yarn less
d be easier to cover.

your project has several pieces, you may
ant to cut them all out before you begin
itching. Keep your cut pieces in a
sealable plastic bag to prevent loss.

EADING THE COLOR KEY

color key is included for each project. The
ey indicates the colors of yarn used and
ow each color is represented on the chart.
or example, when white yarn is
presented by a grey line in the color key,
l grey stitches on the chart should be
itched using white yarn.

HREADING YOUR NEEDLE

any people wonder, "What is the best
ay to thread my needle?" Here are a
ouple of methods. Practice each one with
scrap of yarn and see what works best
r you. There are also several yarn-size
eedle threaders available at your local
aft store.

old Method. First, sharply fold the end of
arn over your needle; then remove needle.
eeping the fold sharp, push the needle
nto the yarn **(Fig. 2)**.

g. 2

hread Method. Fold a 5" piece of sewing
hread in half, forming a loop. Insert loop of
hread through the eye of your needle
Fig. 3). Insert yarn through the loop and
ull the thread back through your needle,
ulling yarn through at the same time.

ig. 3

READING THE CHART

Whenever possible, the drawing on the
chart looks like the completed stitch. For
example, the Tent Stitches on the chart are
drawn diagonally across one intersection of
threads just like Tent Stitches look on your
piece of canvas. Likewise, Gobelin Stitches
on the chart look identical to the Gobelin
Stitches on your canvas. When a stitch
cannot clearly be drawn on the chart, such
as a French Knot, a symbol will be used
instead. If you have difficulty determining
how a particular stitch is worked, refer to
Stitch Diagrams, page 94.

STITCHING THE DESIGN

Securing the First Stitch. Don't knot the end
of your yarn before you begin stitching.
Instead, begin each length of yarn by
coming up from the wrong side of the
canvas and leaving a 1" - 2" tail on the
wrong side. Hold this tail against the
canvas and work the first few stitches over
the tail. When thread is secure, clip the tail
close to your stitched piece. Clipping the
tail closely is important because long tails
can become tangled in future stitches or
show through to the right side of the
canvas.

Using Even Tension. Keep your stitching
tension consistent, with each stitch lying
flat and even on the canvas. Pulling or
yanking the yarn causes the tension to be
too tight, and you will be able to see
through your project. Loose tension is
caused by not pulling the yarn firmly
enough, and the yarn will not lie flat on the
canvas.

Ending Your Stitches. After you've
completed all of the stitches of one color in
an area, end your stitching by running your
needle under several stitches on the back of
the stitched piece. To keep the tails of the
yarn from showing through or becoming
tangled in future stitches, trim the end of the
yarn close to the stitched piece.

Stitching Tips

Length of Yarn. It is best to begin
stitching with a piece of yarn that is
approximately one yard long. However,
when working large areas of the same
color, you may want to begin with a
longer length of yarn to reduce the
number of yarn ends and keep the back
of your project looking neat.

Keeping Stitches Smooth. Most stitches
tend to twist the yarn. Drop your needle
and let the yarn untwist every few
stitches or whenever needed.

JOINING PIECES

Straight Edges. The most common method
of assembling stitched pieces is joining two
or more pieces of canvas along a straight
edge using Overcast Stitches. Place one
piece on top of the other with right or wrong
sides together. Make sure the edges being
joined are even, then stitch the pieces
together through all layers.

Shaded Areas. The shaded area is part of a
chart that has colored shading on top of it.
Shaded areas usually mean that all the
stitches in that area are used to join pieces
of canvas. Do not work the stitches in a
shaded area until your project instructions
say you should.

Stacking. Sometimes pieces need to be
thicker than one layer of canvas. You can
do this by stacking. Before you begin
stitching, follow your project instructions to
stack together plastic canvas pieces so that
the edges are even.

Tacking. To tack pieces, run your needle
under the backs of some stitches on one
stitched piece to secure the yarn. Then run
your needle through the canvas or under
the stitches on the piece to be tacked in
place. The idea is to securely attach your
pieces without your tacking stitches
showing.

Uneven Edges. Sometimes you'll need to
join a diagonal edge to a straight edge. The
holes of the two pieces will not line up
exactly. Just keep the pieces even and
stitch through holes as many times as
necessary to completely cover the canvas.

Unworked Threads. Sometimes you'll need
to join the edge of one piece to an
unworked thread in the center of another
piece. Simply place one piece on top of the
other, matching the indicated threads or
symbols. Join by stitching through both
layers.

WASHING INSTRUCTIONS

If you used washable yarn for all of your
stitches, you may hand-wash plastic
canvas projects in warm water with a mild
soap. Do not rub or scrub stitches; this will
cause the yarn to fuzz. Allow your stitched
piece to air dry. Do not put stitched pieces
in a clothes dryer. The plastic canvas could
melt in the heat of a dryer. Do not dry clean
your plastic canvas. The chemicals used in
dry cleaning could dissolve the plastic
canvas. When piece is dry, you may need
to trim the fuzz from your project with a
small pair of sharp scissors.

Continued on page 94

STITCH DIAGRAMS

Unless otherwise indicated, bring threaded needle up at 1 and all odd numbers and down at 2 and all even numbers.

ALGERIAN EYE STITCH

This stitch forms a square over four threads of canvas. It consists of eight stitches worked in a counterclockwise fashion. Each stitch is worked from the outer edge into the same central hole (**Fig. 4**).

Fig. 4

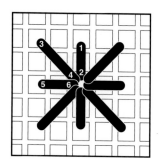

ALICIA LACE STITCH

This series of stitches forms a lacy pattern. It consists of simple rows of Tent and Reversed Tent Stitches (**Fig. 5**).

Fig. 5

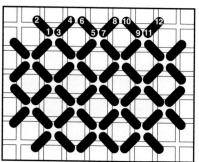

ALTERNATING SCOTCH STITCH

This Scotch Stitch variation is worked over three or more threads, forming alternating blocks (**Fig. 6**).

Fig. 6

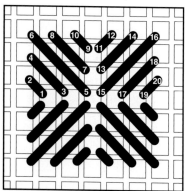

BACKSTITCH

This stitch is worked over completed stitches to outline or define (**Fig. 7**). It is sometimes worked over more than one thread. Backstitch may also be used to cover canvas as shown in **Fig. 8**.

Fig. 7

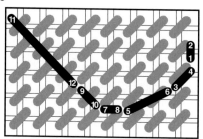

Fig. 8

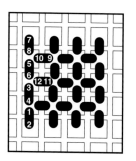

CROSS STITCH

This stitch is composed of two stitches (**Fig. 9**). The top stitch of each cross must always be made in the same direction. The number of intersections may vary according to the chart.

Fig. 9

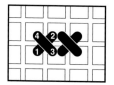

DOUBLE CROSS STITCH

This modification of the Cross Stitch has a star shape (**Fig. 10**).

Fig. 10

ENCROACHING GOBELIN STITCH

This stitch creates a closely woven effe(**Fig. 11**). Each stitch is worked over fo horizontal threads and diagonally over o vertical thread. Each row overlaps t previous row by one thread.

Fig. 11

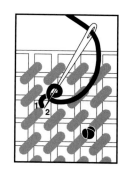

FRENCH KNOT

Bring needle up through hole. Wrap ya once around needle and insert needle same hole or adjacent hole, holding end yarn with non-stitching fingers (**Fig. 12** Tighten knot; then pull needle throug canvas, holding yarn until it must b released.

Fig. 12

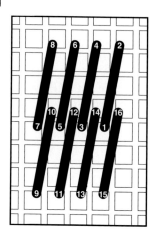

FRINGE STITCH

Fold a length of yarn in half. Thread need with loose ends of yarn. Bring needle up 1, leaving a 1" loop on the back of th canvas. Bring needle around the edge canvas and through loop (**Fig. 13**). Pull t tighten loop (**Fig. 14**). Trim strands t desired length from knot. A dot of glue o back of Fringe will help keep stitches i place.

Fig. 13

Fig. 14

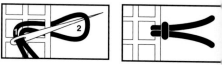

GOBELIN STITCH

This basic straight stitch is worked over two or more threads or intersections. The number of threads or intersections may vary according to the chart (**Fig. 15**).

Fig. 15

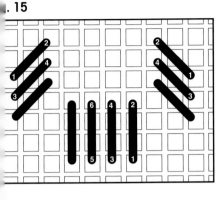

MODIFIED EYELET STITCH

This stitch forms a square over two threads of canvas. It consists of five stitches worked in a clockwise or counterclockwise fashion. Each stitch is worked from the outer edge into the same central hole (**Fig. 16**).

Fig. 16

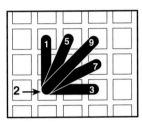

MOSAIC STITCH

This three-stitch pattern forms small squares (**Fig. 17**).

Fig. 17

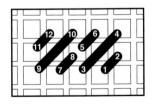

OVERCAST STITCH

This stitch covers the edge of the canvas and joins pieces of canvas (**Fig. 18**). It may be necessary to go through the same hole more than once to get an even coverage on the edge, especially at the corners.

Fig. 18

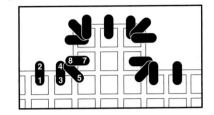

SCOTCH STITCH

This stitch forms a square. It may be worked over three or more horizontal threads by three or more vertical threads. **Fig. 19** shows the Scotch Stitch worked over three threads.

Fig. 19

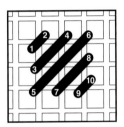

SMYRNA CROSS STITCH

This stitch is worked over two threads as a decorative stitch. Each stitch is worked completely before going on to the next (**Fig. 20**).

Fig. 20

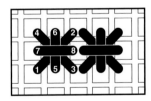

TENT STITCH

This stitch is worked in horizontal or vertical rows over one intersection as shown in **Fig. 21**. Follow **Fig. 22** to work the **Reversed Tent Stitch**. Sometimes when you are working Tent Stitches, the last stitch on the row will look "pulled" on the front of your piece when you are changing directions. To avoid this problem, leave a loop of yarn on the wrong side of the stitched piece after making the last stitch in the row. When making the first stitch in the next row, run your needle through the loop (**Fig. 23**). Gently pull yarn until all stitches are even.

Fig. 21

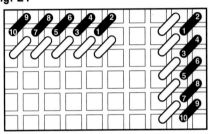

Fig. 22

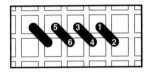

Fig. 23

TURKEY LOOP STITCH

This stitch is composed of locked loops. Bring needle up through hole and back down through same hole, forming a loop on top of the canvas. A locking stitch is then made across the thread directly below or to either side of loop as shown in **Fig. 24**.

Fig. 24

Instructions tested and photography items made by Toni Bowden, Juanita Criswell, Carlene Hodge, Gary Hutcheson, and Patricia McCauley.

INDEX